June Contents

Student Portfolios with Pockets Full of Projects

Additional Resources

June's Special Days

Here are ideas for celebrating some of the other special days in June.

June 2 _____ **Martha Washington's Birthday**
Martha Dandridge Washington was born on June 2, 1732. She married George Washington in 1759 and later became the first First Lady. She was mistress of Washington's Virginia plantation and was also an accomplished weaver, seamstress, gardener, nurse, musician, and cook. How many First Ladies can your students name? Talk about recent First Ladies and their contributions to society.

June 14 _____ **Flag Day**
On June 14, 1777, the Continental Congress made the Stars and Stripes the official flag of the United States. Count the flags you see flying today.

June 16 _____ **First Woman in Space Day**
On June 16, 1963, Valentina V. Tereshkova became the first woman in outer space when she blasted off to make 48 revolutions around the Earth. She operated her ship by manual controls and parachuted to safety when she reentered the Earth's atmosphere after three days in space. Visit the NASA web site and count the number of women who have traveled in space. (http://www.nasa.gov/index.html)

June 18 _____ **International Picnic Day**
Enjoy a picnic today. If it's raining, try a picnic in the gym!

June 21 _____ **Summer Solstice**
In the Northern Hemisphere, the summer solstice falls on or around June 21. This is the longest day of the year and the shortest night because the North Pole is as close to the sun as it ever gets. Note the time the sun sets today. Start a chart to show sunset times for one day a week for several weeks.

June 27 _____ **Helen Keller's Birthday**
Helen Keller was both deaf and blind, yet she became a famous author and lecturer. Recognize the accomplishments of this extraordinary woman by reading one of the biographies describing her life, such as _A Picture Book of Helen Keller_ by David Adler; Holiday House, 1991 or _Helen Keller: Courage in the Dark_ by Johanna Hurwitz; Random Library, 1997.

June 29 _____ **St. Peter's Day**
In Portugal and Brazil fishermen decorate their boats in preparation for St. Peter's Day (São Pedro). There will be joyous music and fireworks as the boats set sail in a floating parade. It's a great day for a lesson on floating and sinking.

June

Sunday	Monday	Tuesday	Wednesday	Thursday	Friday	Saturday

How to Make Pocket Books

Each pocket book has a cover and three or more pockets. Choose construction paper colors that are appropriate to the theme of the book. Using several colors in a book creates an effective presentation.

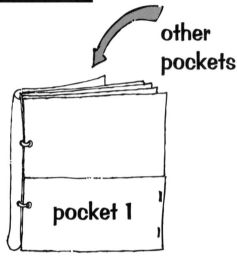

other pockets

pocket 1

Materials

- 12" x 18" (30.5 x 45.5 cm) piece of construction paper for each pocket
- cover as described for each book
- hole punch
- stapler
- string, ribbon, twine, raffia, etc., for ties

Steps to Follow

1. Fold the construction paper to create a pocket. After folding, the paper should measure 12" (30.5 cm) square.

2. Staple the right side of each pocket closed.

3. Punch two or three holes in the left side of each pocket and the cover.

4. Fasten the book together using your choice of material as ties.

5. Glue the poem or information strips onto each pocket as shown on the overview pages of each book.

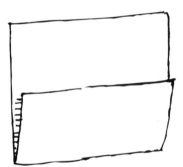

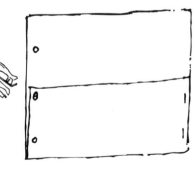

Amazon Rainforest

World Environment Day is June 5. This day, proclaimed by the United Nations, is a great time to begin a unit on a special world environment—the rainforest. This book presents across-the-curriculum activities that help students to learn about the plants and animals of the Amazon rainforest. Students use the information they gather as they create a giant puzzle representing the layers of the rainforest.

Amazon Rainforest

Book Overview _____ **pages 6–8**
These pages show and tell what is in each pocket.

Cover Design _____ **pages 9 and 10**

Pocket Projects _____ **pages 11–34**
Step-by-step directions and patterns for the activities that go in each pocket.

Pocket Labels _____ **pages 35–37**
This poem can also be used for pocket chart activities throughout the month:
- Chant the poem
- Listen for rhyming words
- Learn new vocabulary
- Identify sight words
- Put words or lines in the correct order

Picture Dictionary _____ **page 38**
Use the picture dictionary to introduce new vocabulary and as a spelling reference. Students can add new pictures, labels, and descriptive adjectives to the pages as their vocabulary increases.

Writing Form _____ **page 39**
Use this form for story writing or as a place to record additional vocabulary words.

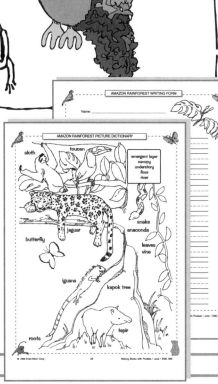

BIBLIOGRAPHY

An Adventure in The Amazon by The Cousteau Society; Simon & Schuster, 1991.
Amazon ABC by Kathy Darling; Lothrop, Lee & Shepard Books, 1996.
The Great Kapok Tree by Lynne Cherry; Harcourt Brace Jovanovich Publishers, 1990.
Journey of the Red-Eyed Tree Frog by Martin and Tanis Jordan; Simon & Schuster, 1991.
Life in the Rainforest by Melvin and Gilda Berger; Hambleton-Hill Publishing, Inc., 1994.
Nature's Green Umbrella, Tropical Rain Forests by Gail Gibbons; Morrow Junior Books, 1994.
Rain Forest by Barbara Taylor; Dorling Kindersley, Inc., 1992.
Rain Forest Babies by Kathy Darling; Scholastic, 1996.
The Tree by Tim Vyner; HarperCollins Publishers, 1994.
A Walk in the Rainforest by Kristin Joy Pratt; Dawn Publications, 1992.
Welcome to the Green House by Jane Yolen; Scholastic, 1993.

POCKET 1

**Amazon
Rainforest Puzzle**   **page 11**
Use these instructions with each pocket to
add a new piece to a rainforest layers puzzle.

**The Emergent
Layer Puzzle Piece**   **page 12**
The first piece of the rainforest layers shows
the tops of the tallest trees peeking through
the dense canopy below.

**Woolly Mouse
Opossum**   **pages 13 and 14**
Your students will love making and learning
about this intriguing creature.

**Emergent Layer
Minibook pages 15 and 16**
Make and read this minibook to find out more
about the emergent layer.

POCKET 2

**The Canopy Layer
Puzzle Piece**   **pages 11 and 17**
The canopy is like the top of a giant umbrella
above the rainforest trees.

Caterpillar to Butterfly   pages 18 and 19
This model transforms from the caterpillar to
the beautiful blue morpho butterfly.

**How the World Looks
to a Sloth**   **page 20**
Students will enjoy hanging upside down on
the playground as part of the prewriting
experience for this writing activity.

Some Sloth!   **page 21**
Use the student "sloth position" photographs
to create a forest of trees, each with a
special sloth.

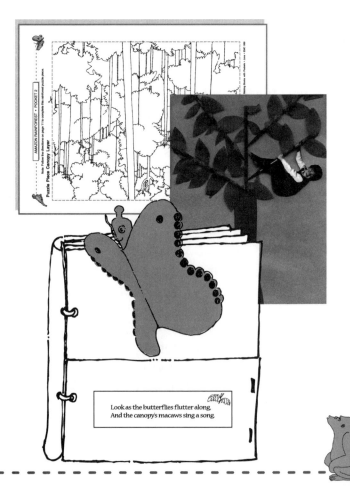

POCKET 3

The Understory Layer
Puzzle Piece   **pages 11 and 22**
The understory of the rainforest is a dark and damp place. Have your students use dark colors to complete this puzzle piece.

A Jungle Vine   **pages 23 and 24**
This trailing vine accompanies a poem that will encourage your students to use descriptive words in their writing.

Draw a Jaguar   **page 25**
Students will enjoy following these steps to draw a jaguar.

POCKET 4

The Rainforest
Floor Puzzle Piece   **pages 11 and 26**
Create another piece for the rainforest puzzle.

Students have made one puzzle piece for each layer of the rainforest. Now they can spread the puzzle pieces on the floor and create a giant cross section of the rainforest.

Ant Farmers   **page 27**
Make a leaf-cutter ant model and discover the important role that the insects of the forest floor play in this rainforest community.

The Kapok Pod   **pages 28 and 29**
Reseeding the rainforest is an ongoing process. Learn about the life cycle of a kapok tree and then write about what you have learned in this pod book.

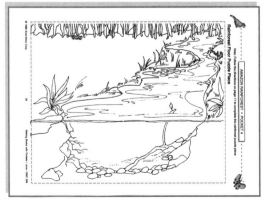

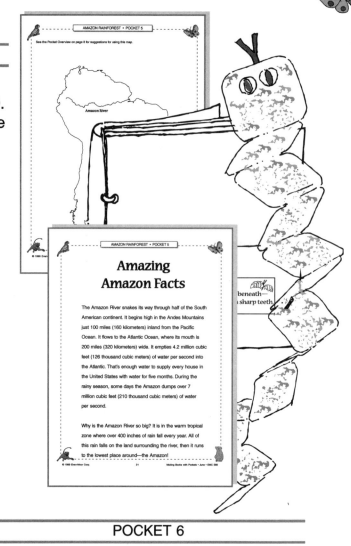

POCKET 5

Map and Facts   **pages 30 and 31**
Make a transparency of the map on page 30.
Review basic map-reading skills as you trace
the Amazon River through South America.
Enjoy reading the Amazing Amazon Facts.

Giant Anaconda   **page 32**
Put ten of these anaconda models together
to see how long a real giant anaconda
would be.

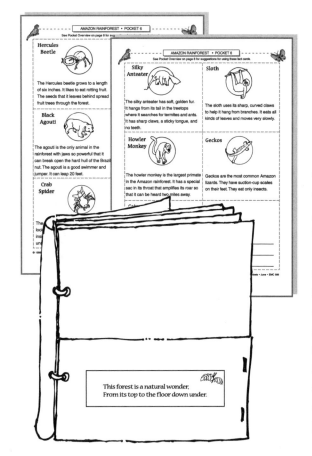

POCKET 6

Animals in the Rainforest
Fact Cards   **pages 33 and 34**
Reproduce the fact cards for individual
students. Have the students cut the cards
apart. Read the facts and then group the
cards according to the layer in which the
animals live. Students can use the blank fact
card to create their own rainforest animal
card. You may want to laminate a classroom
set of fact cards. Punch a hole in the corner
of each card and put the cards on a ring to
make a handy classroom reference.

Materials

- construction paper
  cover—yellow, 12" (30.5 cm) square
  macaw body—red, 11" x 6"
    (28 x 15 cm) rectangle
  beak and feet—yellow scraps
  eye patch—light green scrap
  eye—small white circle
- templates of macaw body parts
  (patterns on page 10)
- thin, black marking pen
- 1" (2.5 cm) squares of colored tissue
  paper—yellow, turquoise, dark blue, red
- glue
- scissors
- pencil

Steps to Follow

1. Make posterboard templates for the macaw body parts,
   using the patterns on page 10.

2. Trace the body template on the red construction
   paper and cut it out.

3. Trace the beak and feet templates on yellow construction
   paper and cut them out.

4. Trace the eye patch template on light green construction paper
   and cut it out.

5. Glue the beak, feet, eye patch, and eye to the body.

6. Draw the center of the eye on the white circle with the black marker.

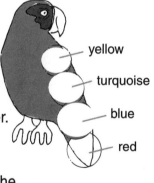

7. Add colorful tissue paper feathers to the wing and tail.
   - Wrap a tissue paper square around the eraser end of a pencil.
   - Dip the eraser end into the glue and then press the eraser onto the
     macaw's wing.
   - Gently remove pencil. The tissue paper square should
     be glued to the wing.
   - Repeat with another tissue paper square.

8. Glue the finished macaw to the yellow cover.

9. Add the title: "The Amazon Rainforest."

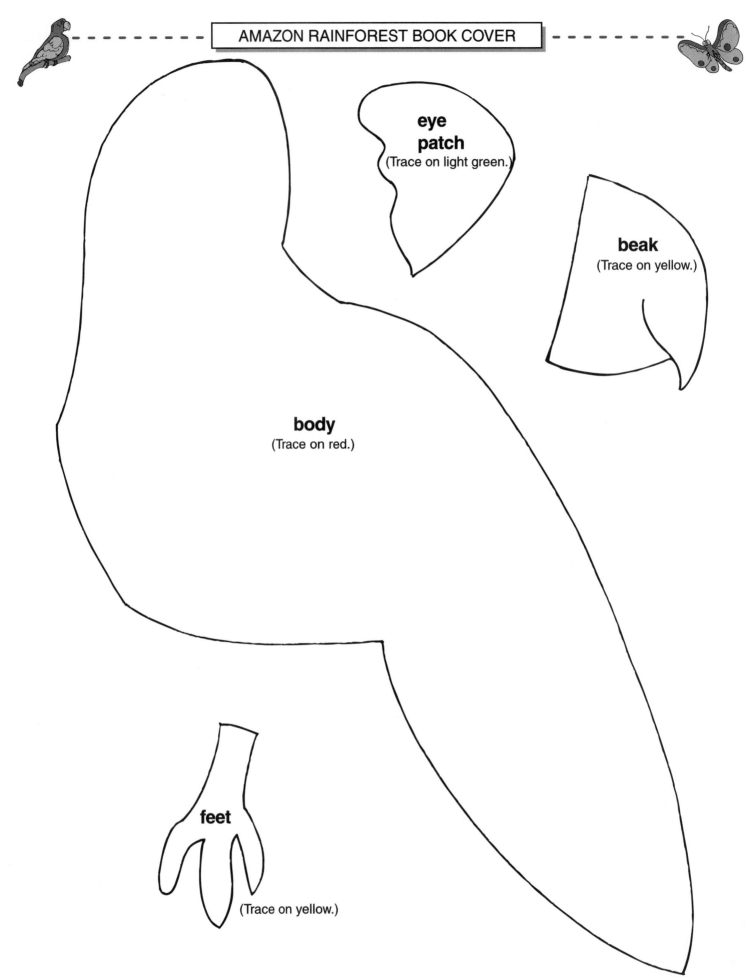

eye patch
(Trace on light green.)

beak
(Trace on yellow.)

body
(Trace on red.)

feet
(Trace on yellow.)

Amazon Rainforest Puzzle

Each pocket of this book will include one puzzle piece representing a layer of the Amazon Rainforest. Follow these steps for the puzzle piece in each pocket. When students have completed all of the puzzle pieces, they will put the puzzle together.

Materials

- puzzle pieces in each pocket, reproduced on white construction paper
- crayons or marking pens
- 8 ½" x 11" (21.5 x 28 cm) posterboard
- glue
- scissors

Steps to Follow

1. Cut out the puzzle piece out along the outline.

2. Color the picture on the puzzle piece.

3. Glue the puzzle piece to the posterboard. Dry completely. Carefully cut out the piece along the puzzle edge.

4. At the end of the activities for each pocket, direct students to write a description of the layer and glue it to the back of the puzzle piece.

5. You may want to make a set of puzzle pieces yourself and laminate them for classroom use.

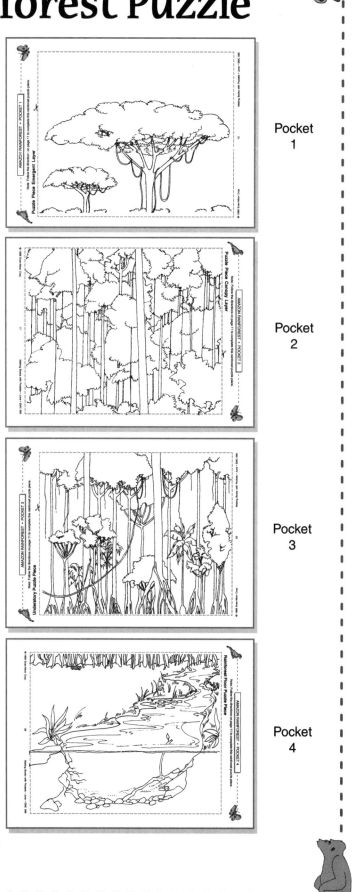

Pocket 1

Pocket 2

Pocket 3

Pocket 4

Note: Follow the directions on page 11 to complete this rainforest puzzle piece.

Emergent Layer Puzzle Piece

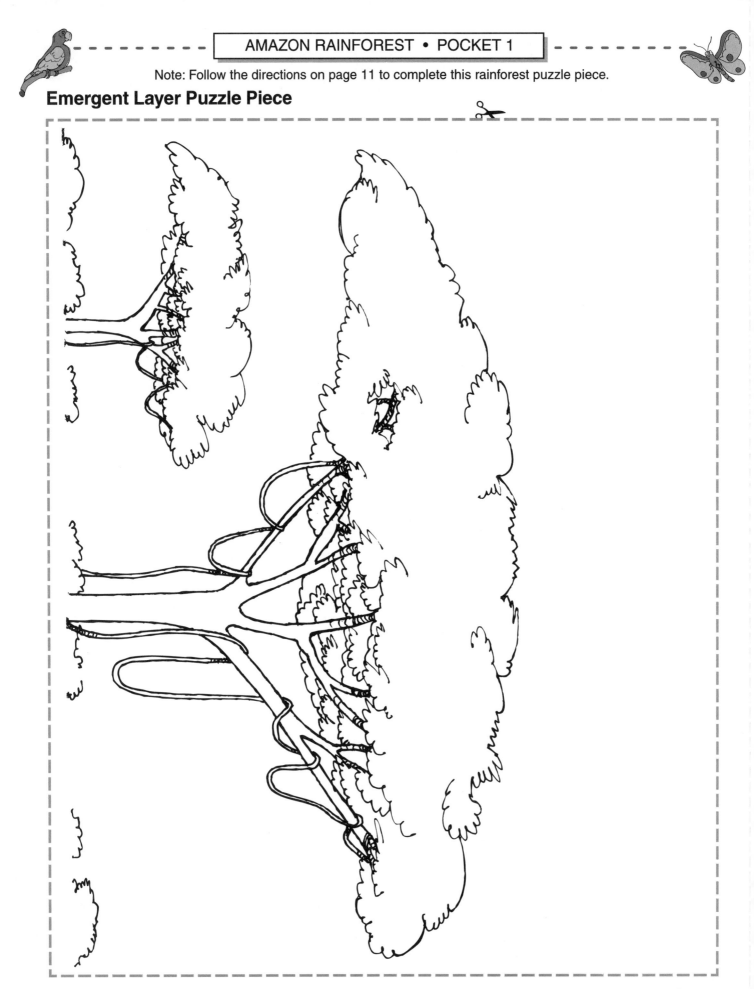

Woolly Mouse Opossum

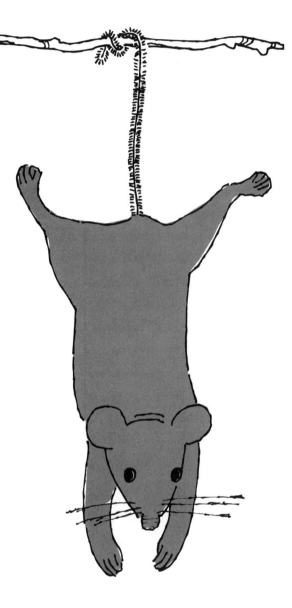

Materials

- woolly mouse opossum pattern on page 14, reproduced on brown paper
- long brown pipe cleaner
- twig
- 2 shiny black beads or buttons
- broom straw, cut into 1" (2.5 cm) pieces
- glue
- tape

Steps to Follow

1. Crumple the brown pattern paper into a ball and then smooth it out again.

2. Cut out the patterns.

3. Glue three edges of the pouch to the belly of the opossum. Do you want to tuck a surprise into the pouch?

4. Glue on the beads for eyes.

5. Glue on the broom straw for whiskers.

6. Tape the pipe cleaner tail in place. Curl the end of the tail around the twig.

Woolly Mouse Opossum Pattern

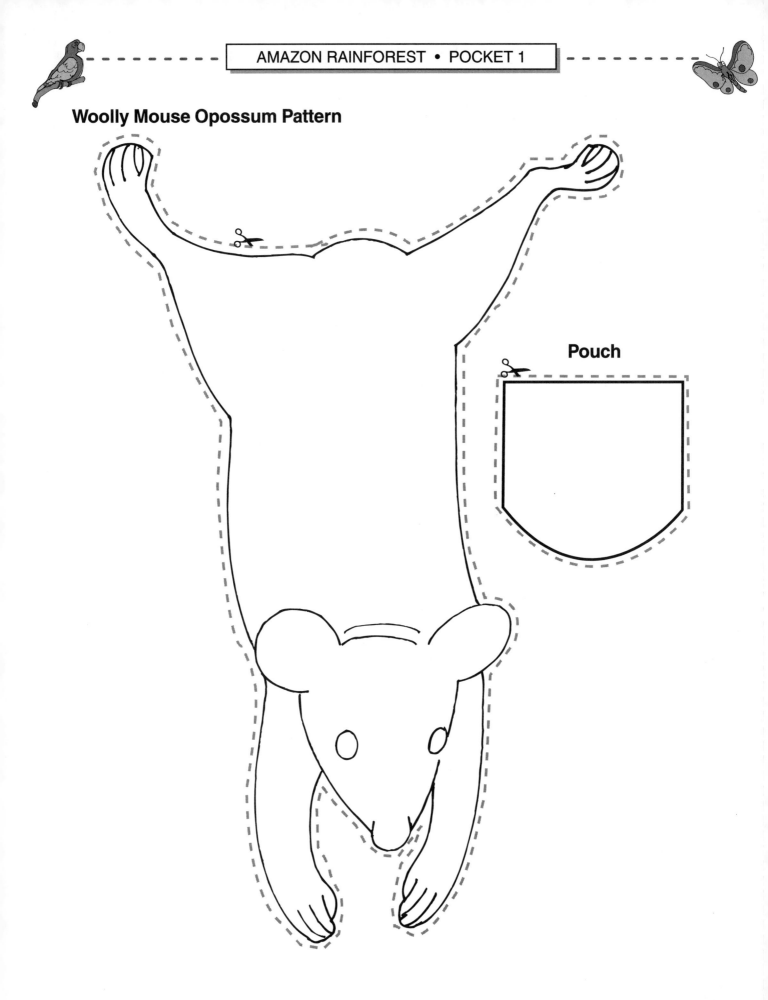

Pouch

Emergent Layer Minibook

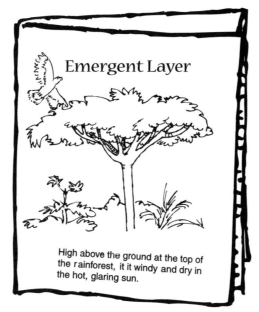

Materials

- minibook on page 16,
  reproduced for students
- crayons or colored marking pens

Steps to Follow

1. Use classroom and library resources to read more about the emergent layer of the rainforest. Start a class chart listing the animals and plants that would be found in this layer. Record additional information as you read.

2. Have students color and fold to make their emergent layer minibooks.

3. Read and discuss the information in the minibook. Add new information to your class chart.

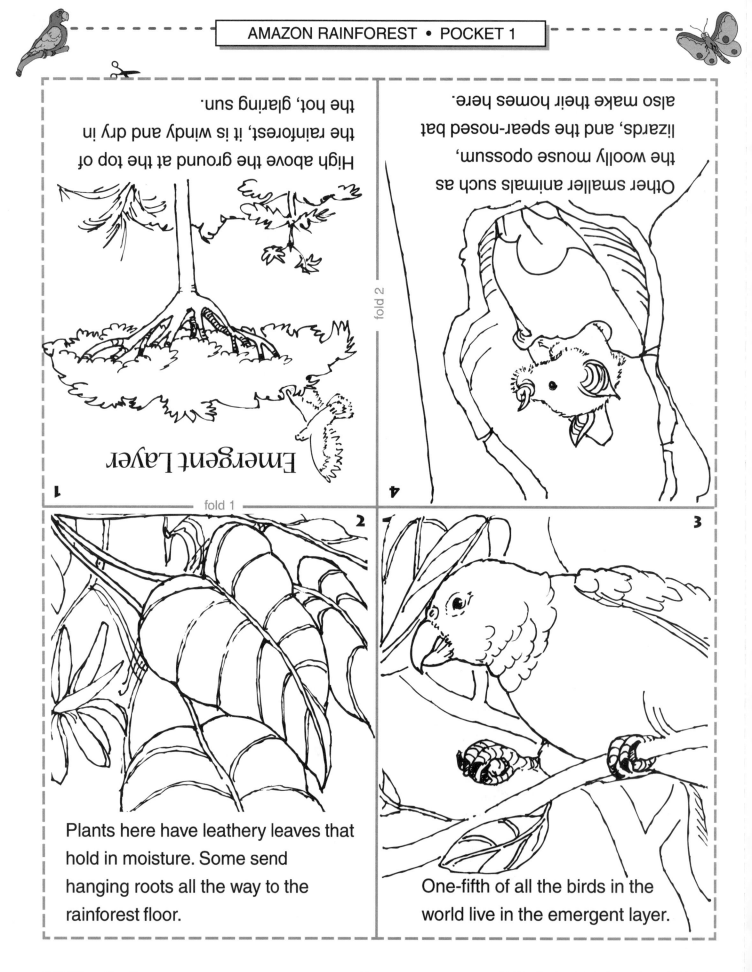

1

Emergent Layer

High above the ground at the top of the rainforest, it is windy and dry in the hot, glaring sun.

4

Other smaller animals such as the woolly mouse opossum, lizards, and the spear-nosed bat also make their homes here.

2

Plants here have leathery leaves that hold in moisture. Some send hanging roots all the way to the rainforest floor.

3

One-fifth of all the birds in the world live in the emergent layer.

fold 1

fold 2

Making Books with Pockets • June • EMC 589

Note: Follow the directions on page 11 to complete this rainforest puzzle piece.

Canopy Layer Puzzle Piece

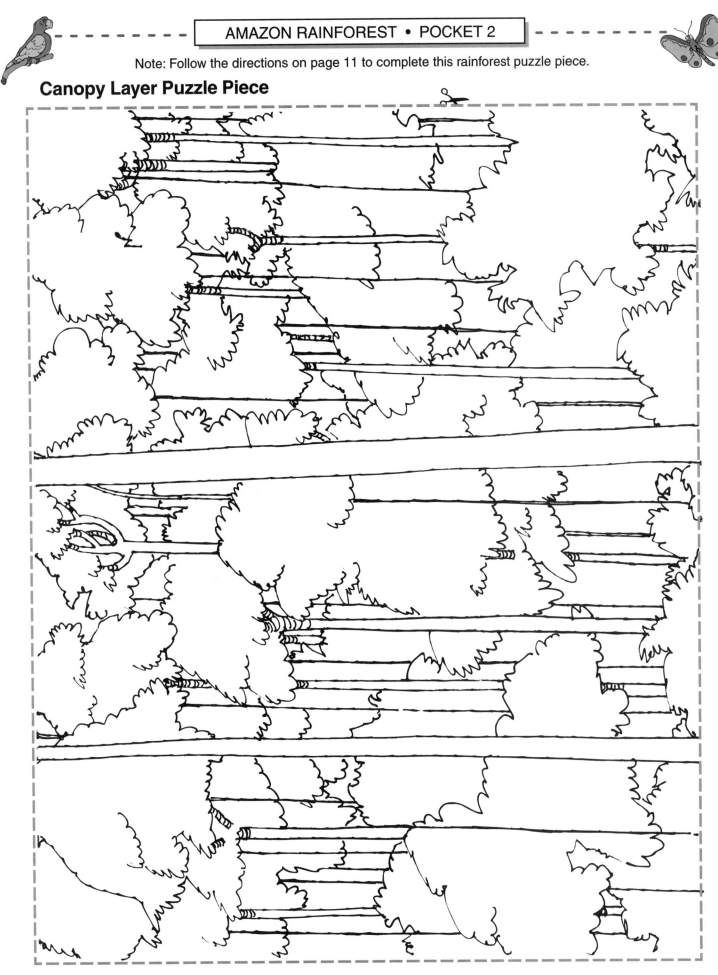

Caterpillar to Butterfly

The blue morpho butterfly lives in the canopy of the Amazon Rainforest. When its wings are folded, the butterfly is brown like the bark on the branches of the trees. When its wings are open, the butterfly is a beautiful, iridescent blue.

Materials

- caterpillar/butterfly pattern on page 19, reproduced on brown construction paper
- bright blue tissue paper cut into small pieces—about ½" x 1" (1.25 x 2.5 cm)
- liquid starch
- paintbrush
- scissors
- black crayon
- glue
- spray glitter

Steps to Follow

1. Cut out the head and the body of the butterfly.

2. Fold the butterfly down the center to make the caterpillar. Color the small bumpy edges black to make caterpillar feet. Draw an eye at one end.

3. Open the caterpillar to make the butterfly. Glue the head between the wings. (The head will fold inside when
the butterfly is folded into the caterpillar.)

4. Lay pieces of blue tissue paper on the wings and brush with liquid starch. Repeat until the wings are a bright blue. Let dry completely. Trim the tissue paper even with the edges of the wings.

5. Spray with glitter.

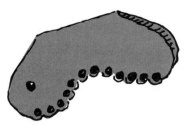

starch

Blue Morpho Pattern

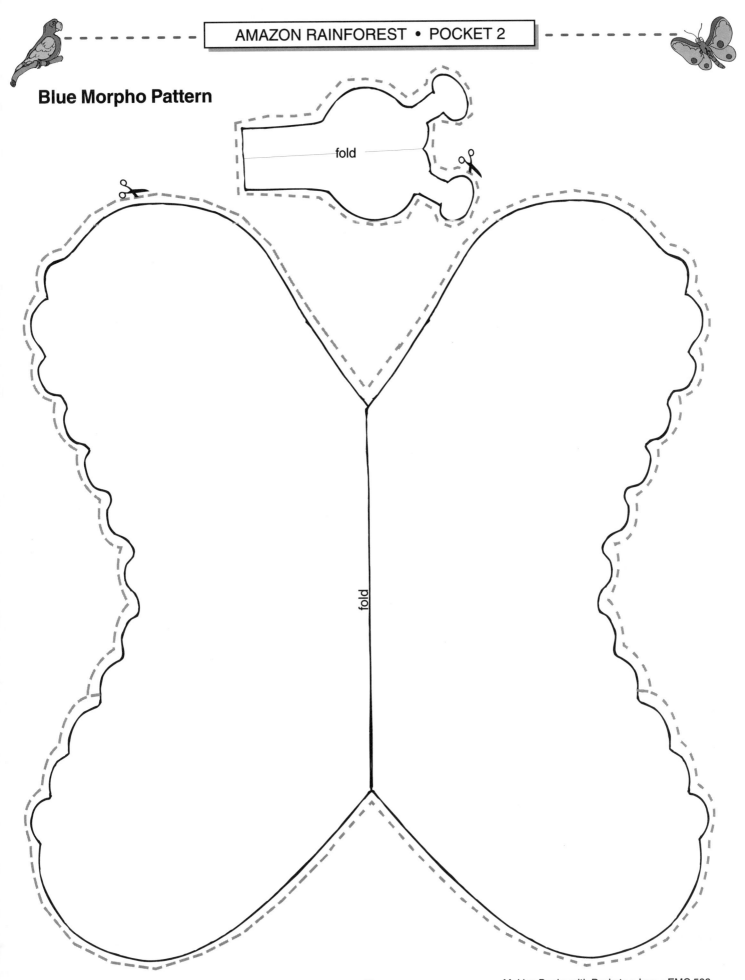

fold

fold

How the World Looks to a Sloth

Look at familiar surroundings from a new perspective and write about your experiences.

Materials

- writing form on page 39, reproduced for students
- monkey bars on the playground
- camera and film

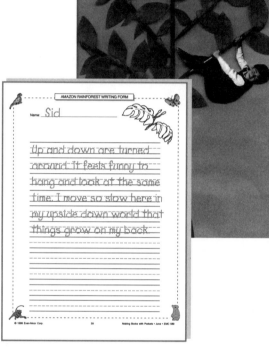

Steps to Follow

1. Ask your students to hang from the monkey bars on your playground as shown and then to describe how this hanging perspective is different from their usual view. Give everyone a chance. Take a picture of each child hanging from the bars.

2. Have students imagine that they are sloths who spend their days hanging upside down in the rainforest canopy. Then students write to describe the rainforest from a sloth's perspective.

3. Glue the finished writing to the back of the "Some Sloth!" project on page 21.

Some Sloth!

Materials

- construction paper
  background—light blue, 9" x 12"
    (23 x 30.5 cm)
  tree trunk—brown, 6½" x 1½"
    (16 x 3.5)
- five 4" (10 cm) wooden skewers or
  sandwich picks, pointed ends cut off
- brown paint
- green tissue paper pieces about
  1" x 2" (2.5 x 5 cm)
- glue
- scissors

Steps to Follow

1. Glue the brown construction paper strip
   to the middle of the light blue construction
   paper so that it resembles a tree trunk.

2. Paint the wooden skewers brown. Let the
   skewers dry completely and then glue
   them onto the top of the tree trunk as shown.

3. Cut leaf shapes from the tissue paper rectangles.
   You will need enough leaves to cover the branches.
   Glue the leaves directly to the skewers. Some of the
   branch parts will show.

4. Cut away the background of the photo of each student,
   leaving only the hanging figure. Glue the figure onto the tree.

Note: Follow the directions on page 11 to complete this rainforest puzzle piece.

Understory Puzzle Piece

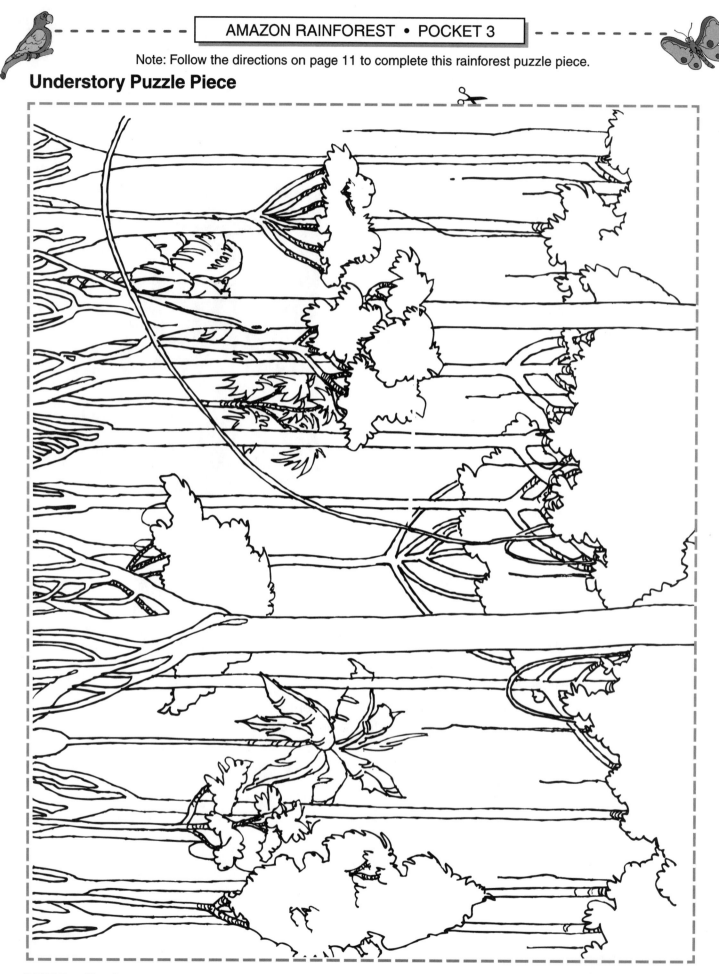

Making Books with Pockets • June • EMC 589

A Jungle Vine

One out of every four plants in the dense understory is a vine. In this activity you will collect verbs that tell what a vine can do, then twist crepe paper into a vine, and write a poem about a jungle vine.

Materials

- leaf pattern on page 24, reproduced on green construction paper
- 10' (3 m) strip cut from a roll of green crepe paper
- hole punch

Steps to Follow

1. Share photographs and illustrations of vines and talk about the vines with your students. If possible, observe growing vines. Brainstorm verbs that describe how a vine moves—climb, twist, hang, fall, cling, swing, grow, dangle, stretch, etc. Record the words that your students suggest in a word bank.

2. Model how to add *ing* to the verbs in the word bank. Write one word on each line of the poem pattern to create a free-verse poem about jungle vines.

    See the vines—

    > *swinging,*
    > *twisting,*
    > *stretching,*
    > *dangling,*
    > *falling—*
    Beautiful jungle vines.

3. Have students write their own poems on the leaves.

4. Punch a hole in the poem leaf. Twist the end of the vine tightly and tie it to the leaf.

5. Twist the crepe paper every six inches, as shown, to make a vine. Hang the vines around your classroom before putting them in Pocket 3 of this book.

See the vines—
swinging,
twisting,
stretching,
dangling,
falling—
Beautiful jungle vines

Poetry Vine Leaf Pattern

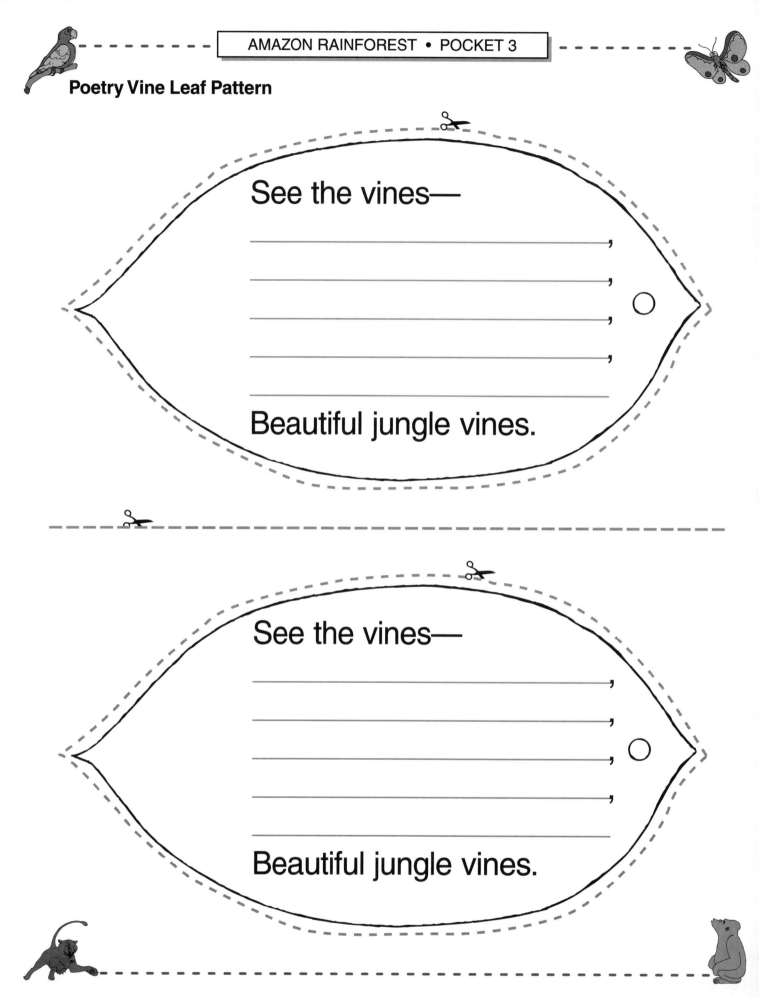

See the vines—

_____,

_____,

_____,

_____,

_____

Beautiful jungle vines.

See the vines—

_____,

_____,

_____,

_____,

_____

Beautiful jungle vines.

Draw a Jaguar

The jaguar is king of the rainforest. At 350 pounds (159 kg), it has no enemies. The jaguar lives alone and hunts at night. It eats lizards, fish, giant otters, deer, and sloths. Its name comes from the Indian word *yaguar*, meaning "he who kills with one leap." Follow these drawing steps to draw a jaguar.

Materials

- 9" x 12" (23 x 30.5 cm) drawing paper
- 9" x 12" (23 x 30.5 cm) dark brown construction paper
- crayons
- watercolor paints
- paintbrush

Steps to Follow

1. Demonstrate the drawing steps on the chalkboard or an overhead as your students follow your instructions. Students will sketch lightly with a pencil, then go over the drawing with heavy crayon strokes. Add spots.

2. Wet your paintbrush and dip into the yellow or orange watercolor paint. Brush the paint across your jaguar. Let the painted jaguar dry completely.

3. Cut out the jaguar. Leave about ½" (2 cm) around the outline.

4. Glue the jaguar to the brown construction paper.

5. Trim the paper in the jaguar shape, leaving a brown border.

Note: Follow the directions on page 11 to complete this rainforest puzzle piece. Point out the jaguar walking on the rainforest floor. It is the correct scale. The trees are huge.

Rainforest Floor Puzzle Piece

Ant Farmers

Read about leaf-cutter ants. There is a good description in the book *Jungles* by Mark Rauzon; Doubleday, 1992.

Materials

- construction paper
  body parts—two red, 4" x 3" (10 x 7.5 cm) pieces
  head—red, 2" (5 cm) square
  legs—six red, 3" x ½" (7.5 x 1.5 cm) strips
  leaf—green, 3" x 4" (7.5 x 10 cm)
- 2" x 3" (5" x 7.5 cm) writing paper
- two black sequins or beans
- two 3" (7.5 cm) pieces of black pipe cleaner
- glue
- scissors

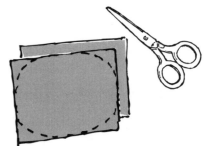

Steps to Follow

1. Round the corners on the two body parts and the head.

2. Glue the three parts together.

3. Glue the pipe cleaner antennae and the sequin or bean eyes to the head.

4. Fold the strips as shown to make the ant's six legs. Glue the legs to the middle body section.

5. Cut a leaf from the green rectangle. Have students write about the leaf-cutter ant's job and glue the writing paper to the leaf. Attach the leaf to the ant model.

The Kapok Pod

Read *The Great Kapok Tree* by Lynne Cherry.
Discuss the life cycle of the kapok tree with your class.

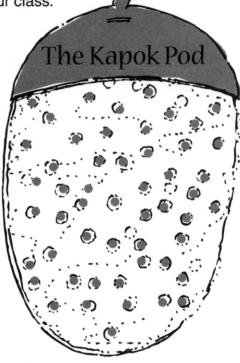

The Kapok Pod

Materials

- kapok pod pattern on page 29, reproduced on white construction paper
- cotton batting
- hole punch
- scraps of brown construction paper
- writing paper
- stapler
- scissors
- glue
- pencil
- brown crayon

Steps to Follow

1. Cut out the kapok pattern. Color the cap brown.

2. Lay the pod on a piece of writing paper and cut a pod shape out of the writing paper.

3. Use the pod pattern to cut the cotton batting.

4. Punch holes from the scraps of brown construction paper. The punched-out holes represent kapok seeds.

5. Glue the seeds to the cotton batting pod.

6. Layer the pieces—the pod with kapok tree facts, the writing paper pod, the cotton batting pod, and the brown cap. Staple through all the layers at the top.

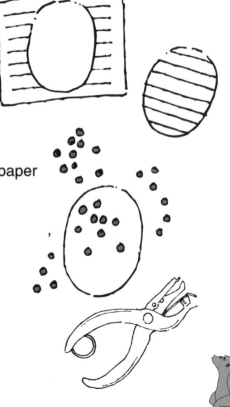

Writing Activities

Students write about the kapok tree in their own words.

Kapok Pattern

pod

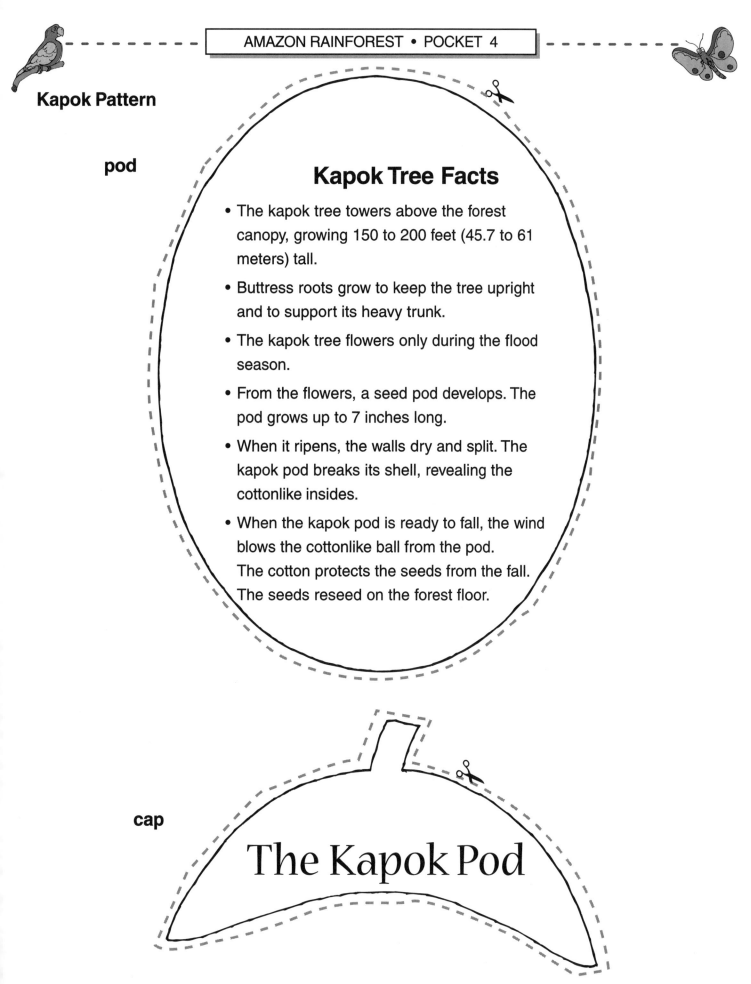

Kapok Tree Facts

- The kapok tree towers above the forest canopy, growing 150 to 200 feet (45.7 to 61 meters) tall.

- Buttress roots grow to keep the tree upright and to support its heavy trunk.

- The kapok tree flowers only during the flood season.

- From the flowers, a seed pod develops. The pod grows up to 7 inches long.

- When it ripens, the walls dry and split. The kapok pod breaks its shell, revealing the cottonlike insides.

- When the kapok pod is ready to fall, the wind blows the cottonlike ball from the pod. The cotton protects the seeds from the fall. The seeds reseed on the forest floor.

cap

The Kapok Pod

See the Pocket Overview on page 8 for suggestions for using this map.

Amazon River

South
America

Amazing Amazon Facts

The Amazon River snakes its way through half of the South American continent. It begins high in the Andes Mountains just 100 miles (160 kilometers) inland from the Pacific Ocean. It flows to the Atlantic Ocean, where its mouth is 200 miles (320 kilometers) wide. It empties 4.2 million cubic feet (126 thousand cubic meters) of water per second into the Atlantic. That's enough water to supply every house in the United States with water for five months. During the rainy season, some days the Amazon dumps over 7 million cubic feet (210 thousand cubic meters) of water per second.

Why is the Amazon River so big? It is in the warm tropical zone where over 400 inches (10 meters) of rain fall every year. All of this rain falls on the land surrounding the river, then it runs to the lowest place around—the Amazon!

Giant Anaconda

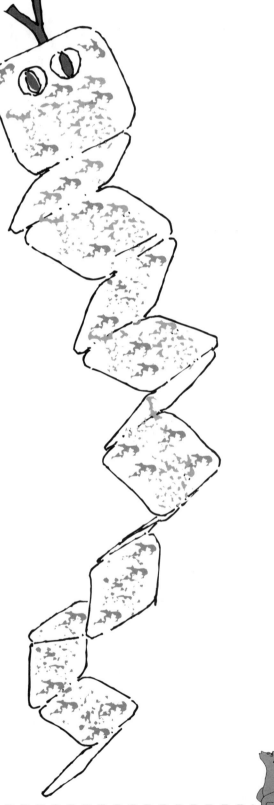

Anacondas of the Amazon grow to 30 feet (9 meters) long—ten times as long as this replica. They weigh over 200 pounds (90 kilograms) and live to be 70 years old. Have ten students put their anacondas end-to-end to see how long a real anaconda is.

Materials

- green, 36" x 5" (91.5 x 13 cm) butcher paper
- scraps of black, white, and red construction paper
- 1" (2.5 cm) square sponge
- green, yellow, and brown paint

Steps to Follow

1. Accordion-fold the strip of butcher paper. Each folded section should be about 4" (10 cm) long. Round the top and bottom edges of the strip.

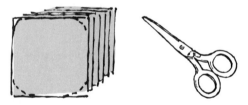

2. Unfold the snake. Sponge paint a pattern on the snake. Use all three colors of paint to create the skin texture. Let the snake dry.

3. Use scraps of white and black to make long oval-shaped eyes. Glue the eyes to the top of the first fold.

4. Make a tongue using red scraps. Glue the tongue onto the backside of the first fold, between the two eyes.

AMAZON RAINFOREST • POCKET 6

See Pocket Overview on page 8 for suggestions for using these fact cards.

Hercules Beetle

The Hercules beetle grows to a length of six inches (15 cm). It likes to eat rotting fruit. The seeds that it leaves behind spread fruit trees through the forest.

Atelopus

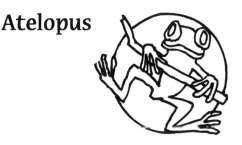

This tiny frog is just 2 ½" (7 cm) long. Its brightly colored skin warns other animals that it is highly poisonous. Even its eggs are poisonous.

Black Agouti

The agouti is the only animal in the rainforest with jaws so powerful that it can break open the hard hull of the Brazil nut. The agouti is a good swimmer and jumper. It can leap 20 feet (about 6 meters).

Fruit-eating Bat

The bats of the rainforest are nocturnal. They navigate by echolocation—making high-pitched sounds and then listening as the sounds bounce back from objects in their way.

Crab Spider

The crab spider is bright yellow and looks like a flower. It sits on a leaf or inside another flower and waits for an unsuspecting bee or fly to hover nearby.

Toucan

The toucan is a colorful bird. Its long, lightweight beak helps it reach fruit from the tips of branches. It sleeps with its beak over its back.

AMAZON RAINFOREST • POCKET 6

See Pocket Overview on page 8 for suggestions for using these fact cards.

Silky Anteater

The silky anteater has soft, golden fur. It hangs from its tail in the treetops where it searches for termites and ants. It has sharp claws, a sticky tongue, and no teeth.

Sloth

The sloth uses its sharp, curved claws to help it hang from branches. It eats all kinds of leaves and moves very slowly.

Howler Monkey

The howler monkey is the largest primate in the Amazon rainforest. It has a special sac in its throat that amplifies its roar so that it can be heard two miles (3.2 km) away.

Geckos

Geckos are the most common Amazon lizards. They have suction-cup scales on their feet. They eat only insects.

Caiman

The caiman is a relative of the alligator and the crocodile. It grows up to 14 feet long (4.3 m) and eats fish.

_____

_____

_____

Note: Reproduce this page and pages 36 and 37 to label each of the six pockets of the Rainforest book.

Pocket 1

From east to west, a brilliant green sea,

See the top of an emerging tree.

Pocket 2

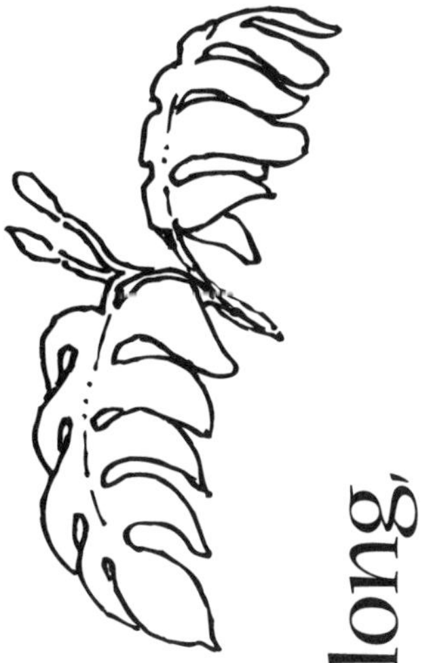

Look as the butterflies flutter along,

And the canopy's macaws sing a song.

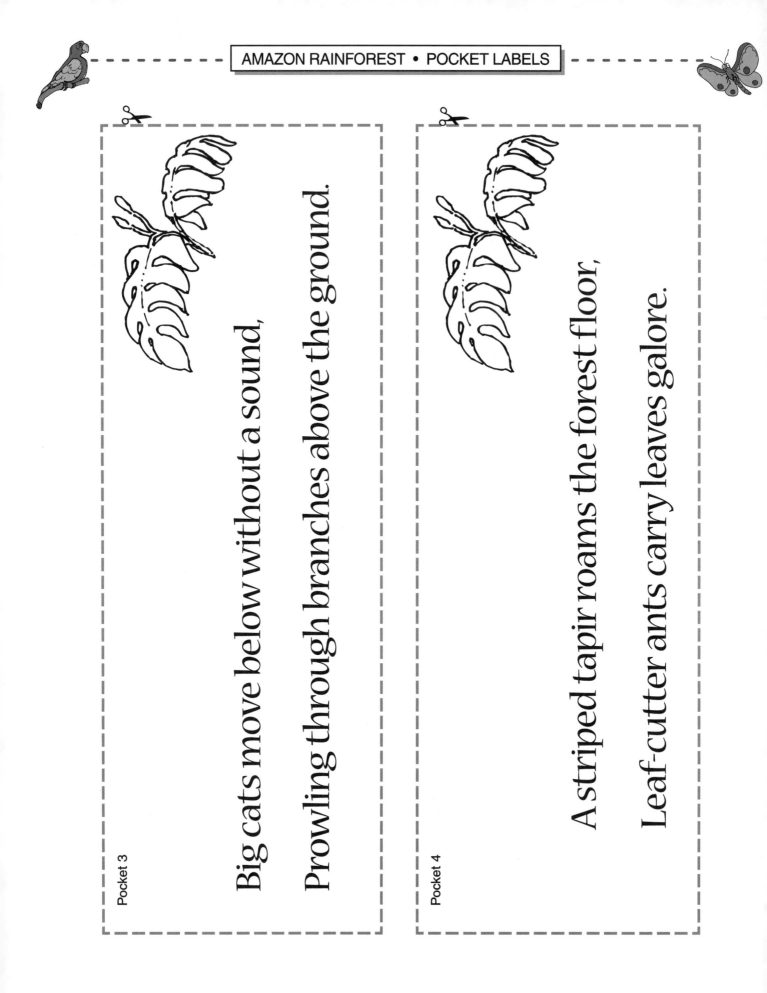

Pocket 3

Big cats move below without a sound,

Prowling through branches above the ground.

Pocket 4

A striped tapir roams the forest floor,

Leaf-cutter ants carry leaves galore.

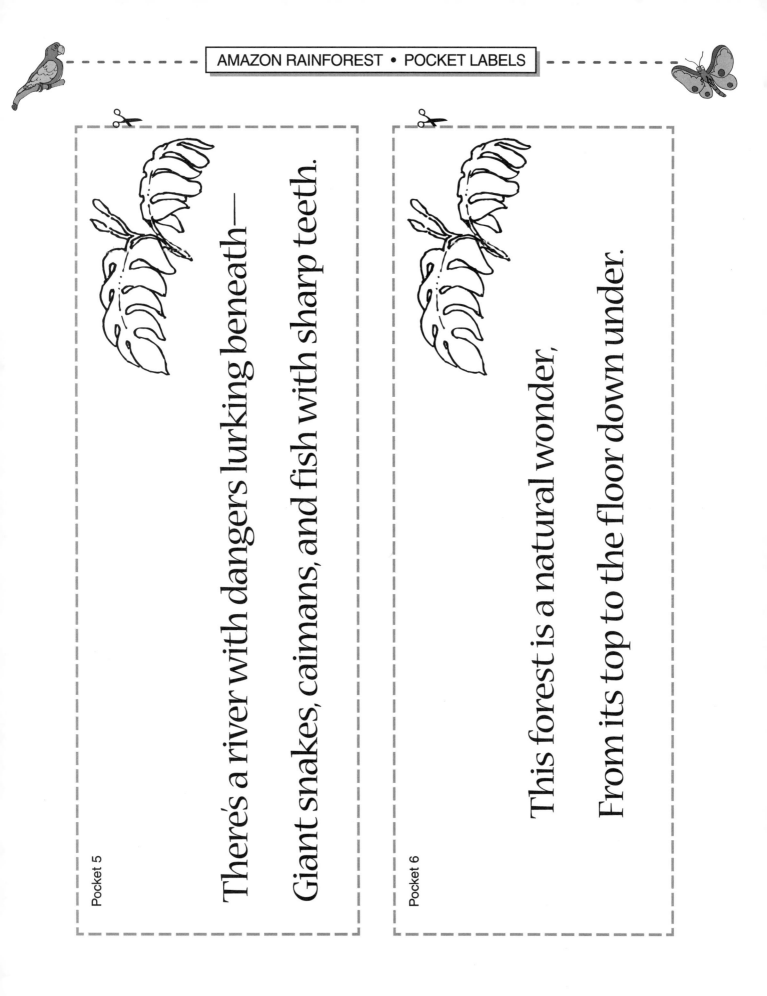

Pocket 5

There's a river with dangers lurking beneath—

Giant snakes, caimans, and fish with sharp teeth.

Pocket 6

This forest is a natural wonder,

From its top to the floor down under.

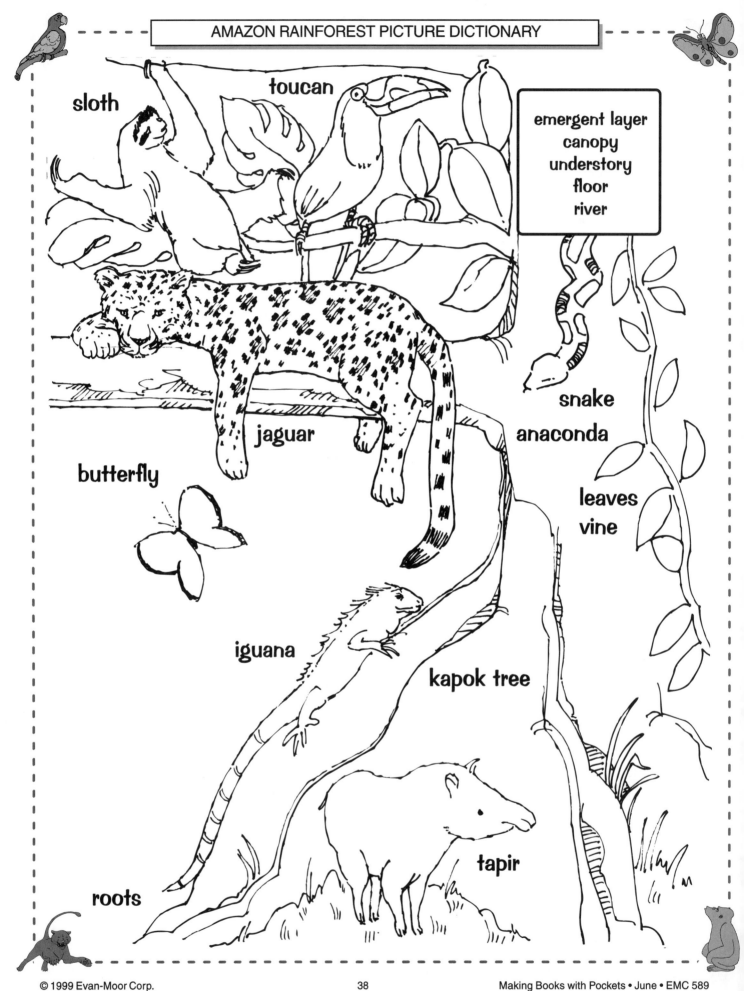

sloth

toucan

emergent layer
canopy
understory
floor
river

jaguar

snake

anaconda

butterfly

leaves

vine

iguana

kapok tree

roots

tapir

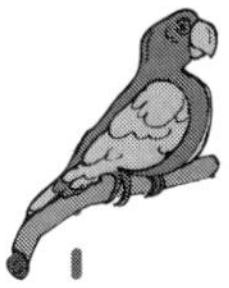

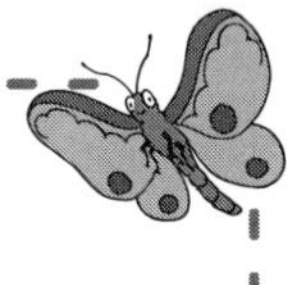

AMAZON RAINFOREST WRITING FORM

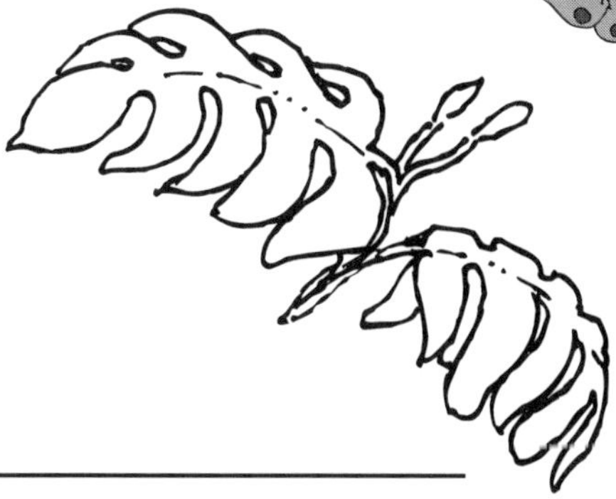

Name: ______________________________

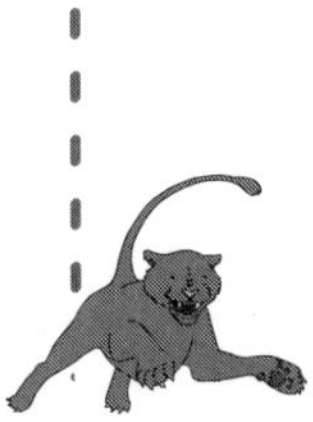

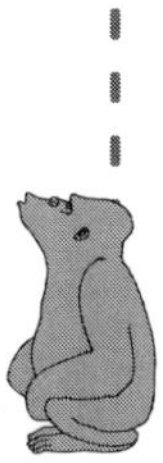

Artists

*C*elebrate the work of six artists. The pocket for each artist includes a teacher information page, a student information bookmark, and an art activity imitating the artist's style. Students write an information bookmark about themselves and select a sample of their own artwork to include in the final pocket.

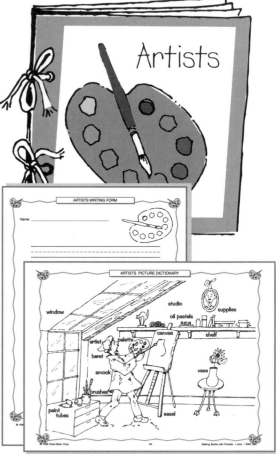

BIBLIOGRAPHY

Books about individual artists are listed on the teacher information page for that artist. The following books address children as artists:

Almost Famous Daisy by Richard Kidd; Simon & Schuster, 1996.

Alvin's Famous No-Horse by William Harry Harding; Henry Holt, 1994.

All I See by Cynthia Rylant; Orchard Books, 1988.

The Art Box by Gail Gibbons; Holiday House, 1998.

The Art Lesson by Tomie De Paolo; Putnam Publishing, 1989.

The Fantastic Drawings of Danielle by Barbara McClintock; Houghton Mifflin, 1996.

I Am an Artist by Pat Lowery Collins; Millbrook Press, 1994.

Painted Dreams by Karen Lynn Williams; Lothrop, Lee & Shepard, 1998.

The Painter by Peter Catalanotto; Orchard Books, 1995.

POCKET 1

Henri Matisse
Information Pages   pages 45 and 46
Read the books about Matisse listed in the bibliography on page 45 and show photographs of some of his works. Use the information page as a resource to help answer student questions. Students add interesting facts to the Matisse bookmark, cut it out, and put it in this pocket.

A Movement Collage   page 47
Students create a colorful checkerboard background, then cut shapes and glue them to the background to represent movement.

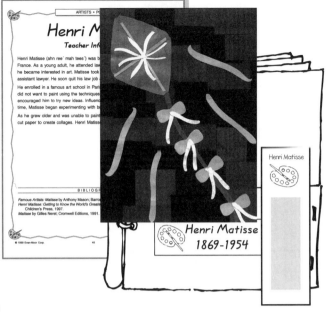

POCKET 2

Claude Monet
Information Pages   pages 48 and 49
Take a walk to a quiet spot outdoors and tell your students about Monet's love of the changing light and seasons. Use the information page, classroom books, and library resources to complete the Monet bookmark.

Monet's Haystacks   page 50
Students imitate Monet's style to make their own "Haystacks" painting.

POCKET 3

Georgia O'Keeffe
Information Pages   pages 51 and 52
Show your students some of Georgia O'Keeffe's big, bold flowers as you read to learn about her art. Students can illustrate the bookmark about her life with boldly colored flowers after adding some interesting facts.

Tissue Paper
Flower Collage   page 53
Students use bright tissue paper to create a big flower collage.

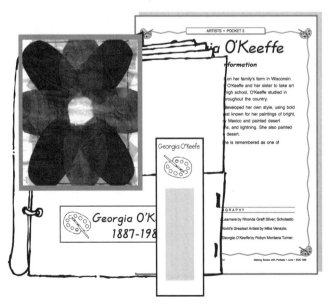

Pablo Picasso
1840-1926

POCKET 4

Pablo Picasso
Information Pages   pages 54 and 55
Enjoy examples of the different kinds of art that Pablo Picasso created as you learn about his life. Several excellent children's biographies are listed on page 54. Students will add to the highlights of his life on the artist bookmark.

Picasso Portrait   page 56
Students paint a self-portrait with poster paint, cut the portrait into pieces, and glue it back together to create their own "Picassos."

POCKET 5

Diego Rivera
Information Pages   pages 57 and 58
Introduce the mural as an art form when you read and learn about Diego Rivera. Suggest that students find murals in your community. Compare those murals with Rivera's murals. Complete the Rivera bookmark.

A Mural of Student Life   page 59
Students draw and paint a mural representing their everyday lives. Fill a wall with the completed murals for a colorful salute to Rivera before putting the murals in this pocket.

Diego Rivera
1886-1957

POCKET 6

Another
Important Artist   page 60 and 61
Students complete an information bookmark about themselves and choose a sample of their artwork to put in this pocket.

Materials

- palette template and paintbrush pattern, on page 44
- construction paper
  book cover—light brown, 12" (30.5 cm) square
    white, 11" (28 cm) square
  palette—black, 10" x 8" (25.5 x 20 cm) rectangle
  paint splotches—1½" (3.5 cm) squares of red, orange, yellow, green, blue, purple
- glue
- scissors
- black crayon or marking pen
- chalk or light crayon

Steps to Follow

1. Glue the white square inside the light brown square, leaving a narrow brown border on all sides.

2. Trace the palette template onto the black paper rectangle, using chalk or a light crayon. Cut out the palette. Cut out the thumb hole.

3. Glue the black palette to the cover.

4. Tear paint splotches from each of the color scraps. Glue the splotches to the palette.

5. Color the paintbrush and cut it out. Glue the brush to the palette.

7. Write "Artists" across the top of the cover.

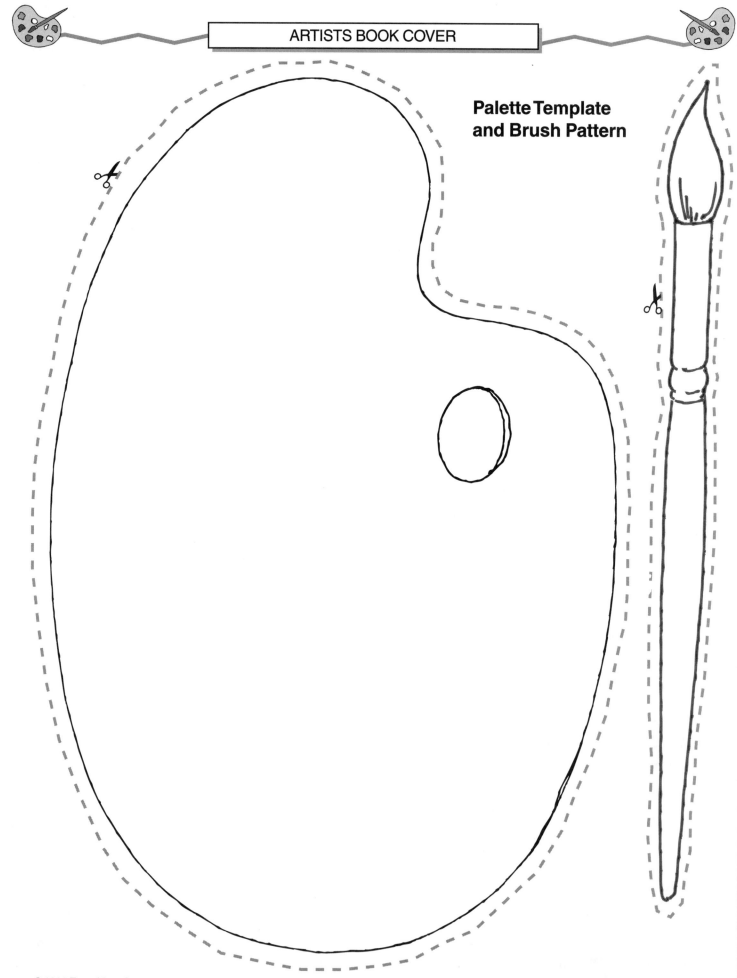

Palette Template and Brush Pattern

Henri Matisse
Teacher Information

Henri Matisse (ahn ree´ mah tees´) was born in 1869 in Le Cateau-Cambresis, France. As a young adult, he attended law school. When he was 20 years old, he became interested in art. Matisse took art classes while working as an assistant lawyer. He soon quit his law job and devoted all his time to art.

He enrolled in a famous art school in Paris, France. He soon realized that he did not want to paint using the techniques he was learning. One of his teachers encouraged him to try new ideas. Influenced by other Impressionists of the time, Matisse began experimenting with bright spots of color.

As he grew older and was unable to paint, Matisse continued his art by using cut paper to create collages. Henri Matisse died when he was 84.

BIBLIOGRAPHY

Famous Artists: Matisse by Anthony Mason; Barrons, 1995.
Henri Matisse: Getting to Know the World's Greatest Artists by Mike Venezia; Children's Press, 1997.
Matisse by Gilles Neret; Cromwell Editions, 1991.

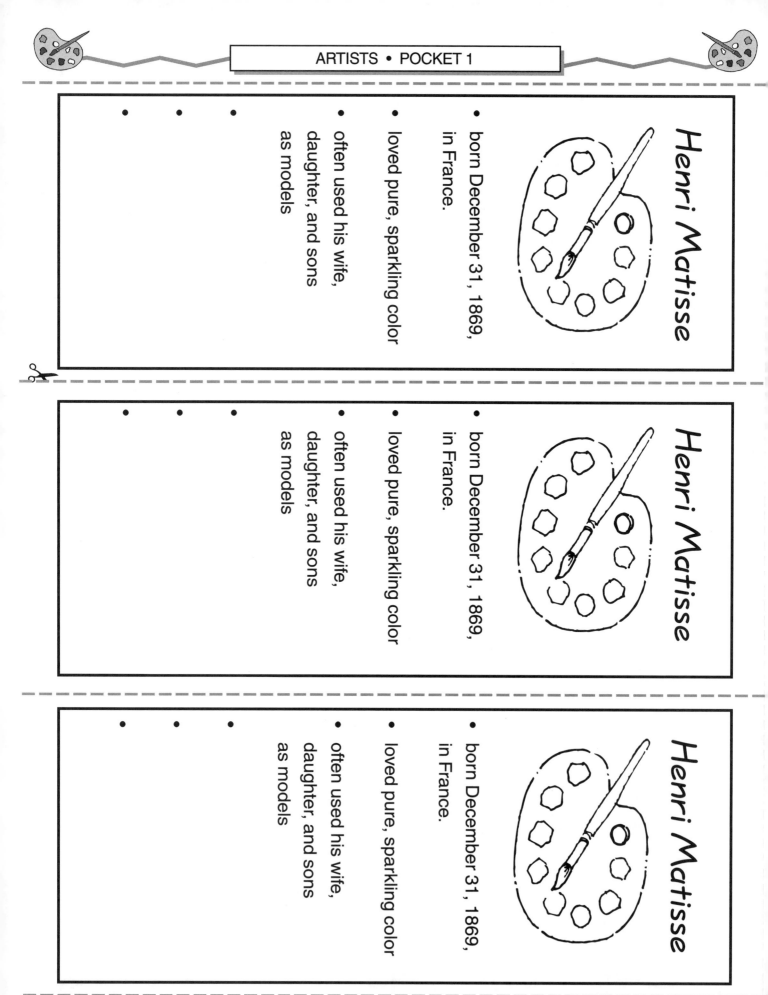

Henri Matisse

- born December 31, 1869, in France.
- loved pure, sparkling color
- often used his wife, daughter, and sons as models

Henri Matisse

- born December 31, 1869, in France.
- loved pure, sparkling color
- often used his wife, daughter, and sons as models

Henri Matisse

- born December 31, 1869, in France.
- loved pure, sparkling color
- often used his wife, daughter, and sons as models

A Movement Collage

"Creole Dancer" is a famous collage inspired by dancer Katherine Dunham. When Matisse created this collage, he used a background that is a colorful, irregular checkerboard. He placed contrasting curved shapes on the checkerboard to symbolize the moving dancer.

Preparing for the lesson

As a class, think about things that move. List the things on a piece of chart paper. This list of moving things will help students think of subjects they might use for their collages.

Materials

- construction paper
  base of collage—9" x 12" (23 x 30.5 cm) sheet, any color
  checkerboard—small squares and rectangles, many bright colors
  moving object—scraps of construction paper, many colors

- scissors

- glue

Steps to Follow

1. Glue small squares and rectangles onto the construction paper background. The background should become an irregular checkerboard. Avoid gluing two rectangles of the same color next to each other or creating patterns.

2. Think of a thing that moves. (Have students use the chart paper list to help them decide.)

3. Cut construction paper scraps into shapes that represent the object. Cut a few smaller shapes to indicate movement.

4. Glue these shapes to the checkerboard background.

Claude Monet
Teacher Information

Claude Monet (clohd moh nay´) was born in 1840 in Paris, France. As a young teenager, he drew caricatures of people as a job. At 22, Monet enrolled in art school in Paris. While he was there, he met other artists such as Pierre-Auguste Renoir, Alfred Sisley, and Frédéric Bazille. They often painted together in the countryside. Claude Monet was especially fond of the water. He painted many pictures of oceans, lakes, ponds, and boats.

When Monet grew older, he moved to Giverny (Zhee´ vair nee´), a small town. There he built a beautiful water garden which became the subject of many of his paintings. Monet often painted the same subjects, such as haystacks, water lilies, and the Japanese footbridge in his water garden at different times of the day and year, showing the changing seasons and the changing light.

Claude Monet died at 86. He is known today as one of the world's greatest impressionistic artists.

BIBLIOGRAPHY

Claude Monet: Getting to Know the World's Greatest Artists by Mike Venezia; Children's Press, 1993.
Claude Monet: The Magician of Color; Prestel Books, 1997.
Famous Artists: Monet by Anthony Mason; Barron's, 1995.
The Impressionists by Gilles Neret; Tiger Books International, 1992.
Landscapes by Penny King and Clare Randhill; Crabtree Publishing Co., 1992.
Linnea in Monet's Garden by Christina Bjork and Lena Anderson; R & S Books, 1987.
Once Upon a Lily Pad: Froggy Love in Monet's Garden by Joan Sweeney; Chronicle Books, 1995.

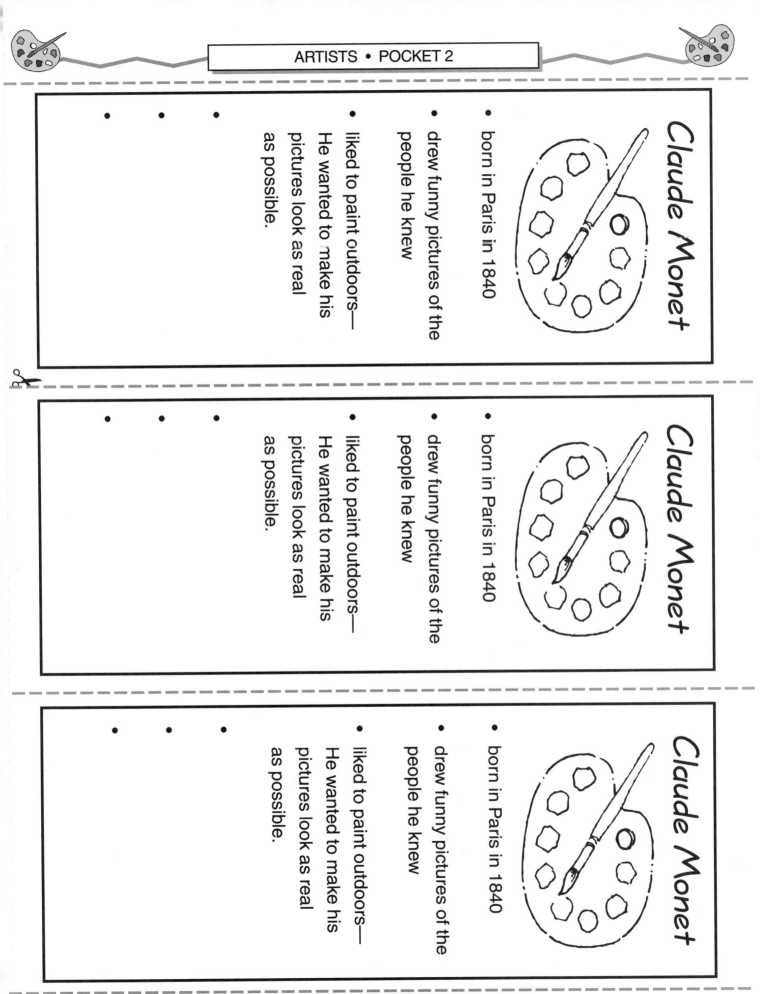

Claude Monet

- born in Paris in 1840

- drew funny pictures of the people he knew

- liked to paint outdoors— He wanted to make his pictures look as real as possible.

Claude Monet

- born in Paris in 1840

- drew funny pictures of the people he knew

- liked to paint outdoors— He wanted to make his pictures look as real as possible.

Claude Monet

- born in Paris in 1840

- drew funny pictures of the people he knew

- liked to paint outdoors— He wanted to make his pictures look as real as possible.

Monet's Haystacks

The "Haystack" series is a well-known set of paintings done by Monet. Each painting in the series is painted at a different time of day so the paintings differ in shadow, placement, and intensity of color. This project is a reproduction of one painting from the series.

Materials

- 9" x 12" (23 x 30.5 cm) light blue construction paper
- tempera paint—light green, white, light orange, yellow, and lavender
- plate to hold paint
- paintbrush
- paper towel
- water

Steps to Follow

For this activity, the teacher will demonstrate each step, pausing as students complete the step. Brushes should be cleaned when changing colors.

1. Place the light blue construction paper crosswise on the work surface. Paint the foreground first. Dip the side of the paintbrush bristles in light orange paint. Dab the paint on the bottom third of the paper. Use an up and down motion, not a back and forth stroke. The paint should have a textured surface. Do not cover the foreground completely.

2. Dip the brush in lavender paint. Dab the brush on the paper to make a hill that fills the next third of the paper.

3. Dab yellow and white paint on the remaining blue paper to make the sky.

4. Let the painting dry before adding additional details.

5. Dab light green along the base of the purple hill.

6. Dab yellow paint to make two haystacks in the foreground of the picture.

7. Dab shadows in front of the haystacks with lavender paint.

8. Allow your painting to dry completely.

Georgia O'Keeffe

Teacher Information

Georgia O'Keeffe was born in 1887 on her family's farm in Wisconsin. O'Keeffe's mother encouraged both O'Keeffe and her sister to take art lessons. After she graduated from high school, O'Keeffe studied in various art schools and colleges throughout the country.

As Georgia O'Keeffe painted, she developed her own style, using bold shapes and bright colors. She is best known for her paintings of bright, colorful flowers. She moved to New Mexico and painted desert scenes with bright suns, dust storms, and lightning. She also painted animal bones that she found in the desert.

Georgia O'Keeffe lived to be 98. She is remembered as one of America's greatest artists.

BIBLIOGRAPHY

Exploring Art Masterpieces With Young Learners by Rhonda Graff Silver; Scholastic Professional Books, 1996.

Georgia O'Keeffe: Getting to Know the World's Greatest Artists by Mike Venezia; Children's Press, 1993.

Portraits of Women Artists for Children: Georgia O'Keeffe by Robyn Montana Turner; Little, Brown and Co., 1991.

Georgia O'Keeffe

- born in Sun Prairie, Wisconsin, in 1887
- used bright colors and bold shapes
- received the Medal of Freedom and the National Medal of Arts

Georgia O'Keeffe

- born in Sun Prairie, Wisconsin, in 1887
- used bright colors and bold shapes
- received the Medal of Freedom and the National Medal of Arts

Georgia O'Keeffe

- born in Sun Prairie, Wisconsin, in 1887
- used bright colors and bold shapes
- received the Medal of Freedom and the National Medal of Arts

Tissue Paper Flower Collage

Georgia O'Keefe painted beautiful bold flowers. Her flowers filled the canvases. In this project students will create bright tissue paper flowers, then cut away the background to leave only the flower.

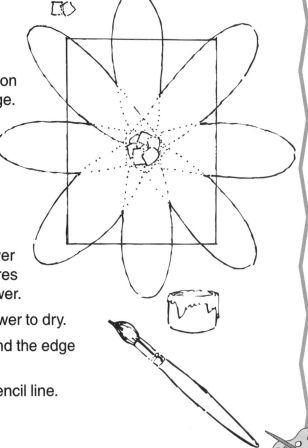

Materials

- 9" x 12" (23 x 30 cm) white construction paper
- eight or more 4" x 5" (10 x 13 cm) pieces of tissue paper in assorted colors
- scissors
- liquid starch
- paintbrush
- 8" x 11" (20 x 28 cm) piece of posterboard

Steps to Follow

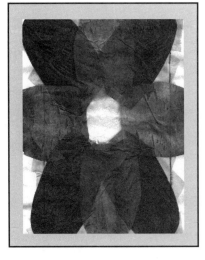

1. Choose two colors of tissue paper for the flower petals. You will need four pieces of each color. Round one end of the tissue paper to make petal shapes. Arrange the petals on the white construction paper rectangle. Petal edges may hang off the page.

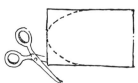

2. Choose a different color of tissue paper for the flower center. Cut the center tissue paper into small squares and arrange the squares to fill the center of the flower.

3. Paint starch over the tissue paper and allow the flower to dry.

4. Center the posterboard over the flower. Trace around the edge lightly with a pencil.

5. Trim off the edges of the flower picture along the pencil line.

Pablo Picasso

Teacher Information

Pablo Picasso was born in 1881 in Málaga, Spain. His father was an art teacher. At a young age, Picasso was encouraged to draw and paint.

When he was 19, Picasso went to Paris, France, where he continued to paint. During this time a close friend of his died. His friend's death made him sad and his art reflected this sadness. He painted with blue colors, showing sad and lonely people. This was a very depressing time for him. Later, this period of Picasso's life became known as his Blue Period.

A few years later Picasso changed his colors and subjects. He began painting brighter, happier things such as the clowns from the circus. This was the beginning of his Rose Period.

Picasso soon changed his style again. He developed a new style called Cubism and added new texture to his paintings and collages.

Picasso lived to be 92. He is remembered for his paintings, sculptures, and ceramics. His work and influence are very important to Modern Art.

BIBLIOGRAPHY

Pablo Picasso by Ibi Lepscky; Barrons Juveniles, 1993.
Picasso by Anthony Mason; Barrons Juveniles, 1995.
Picasso by Mike Venezia; Children's Press, 1988.
Picasso: Breaking the Rules of Art by David Spence; Barrons Educational
    Series, 1997.
When Pigasso Met Mootisse by Nina Laden; Chronicle Books, 1998.

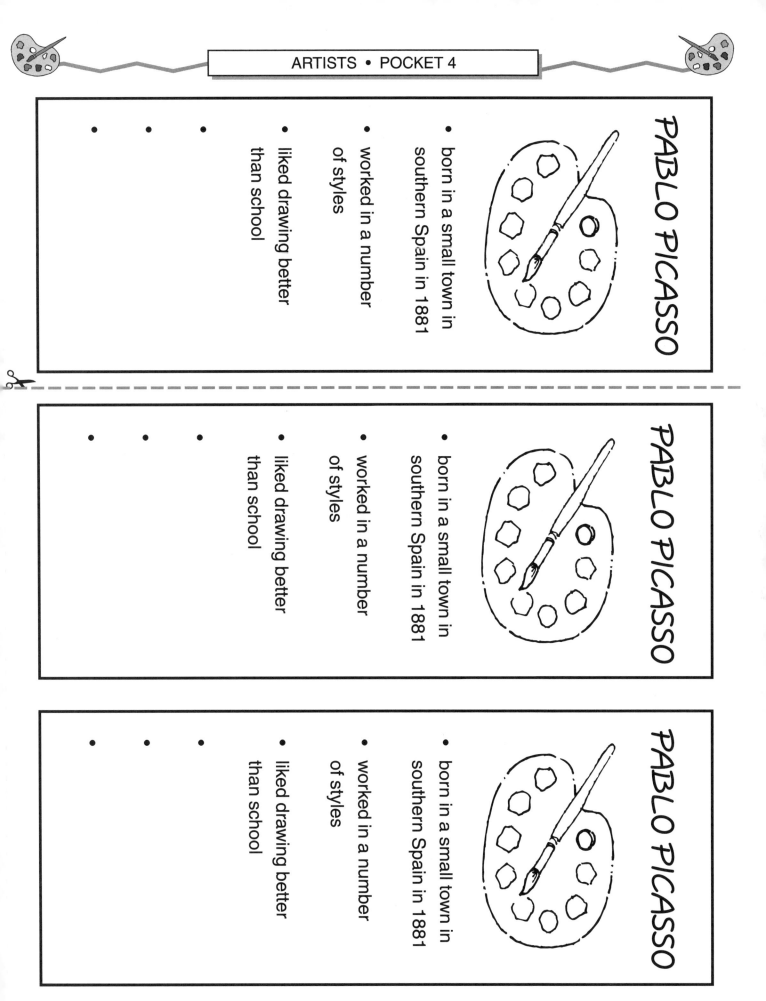

PABLO PICASSO

- born in a small town in southern Spain in 1881
- worked in a number of styles
- liked drawing better than school

PABLO PICASSO

- born in a small town in southern Spain in 1881
- worked in a number of styles
- liked drawing better than school

PABLO PICASSO

- born in a small town in southern Spain in 1881
- worked in a number of styles
- liked drawing better than school

Picasso Portrait

Students cut the portrait they paint into puzzle pieces and then glue them onto a background to create their own original "Picassos."

Materials

- construction paper
  face—white, 9" x 12"
     (23 x 30.5 cm)
  background—black, 9" x 12"
     (23 x 30.5 cm)
- poster paint
- paintbrush
- scissors
- glue

Steps to Follow

1. Paint a face on the white rectangle. Fill the whole space.

2. Let the painting dry completely.

3. Cut out the face. Throw away the scraps.

4. Cut the face into pieces.

5. Glue the face pieces to the black paper. Leave some space between the pieces and glue them to the paper at different angles.

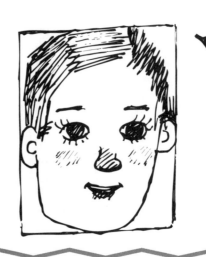

Diego Rivera

Teacher Information

Diego Rivera was born in 1886 in Guanajuato, Mexico. As a young child, he had a great imagination and many times he painted pictures on the walls of his home. Rivera's parents sent him to the San Carlos Art Academy, a famous art academy in Mexico City.

Diego Rivera soon developed his own style of painting. He painted everyday scenes of Mexican life. He wanted his paintings to be seen by everyone, not just the very wealthy. So Rivera painted murals on the walls of churches, schools, hospitals, government buildings, and hotels. He usually painted on wet plaster. (These murals are called frescos.)

Diego Rivera lived to be 71. A few of his murals are in America, however most are in Mexico. Many of his murals tell the stories of people and their day-to-day lives. They reflect his feelings of respect for the hard working, common people. His murals were painted for these people.

BIBLIOGRAPHY

Diego by Jeanette Winter; Alfred A. Knopf, 1991.
Diego Rivera: Getting to Know the World's Greatest Artists by Mike Venezia; Children's Press, 1994.

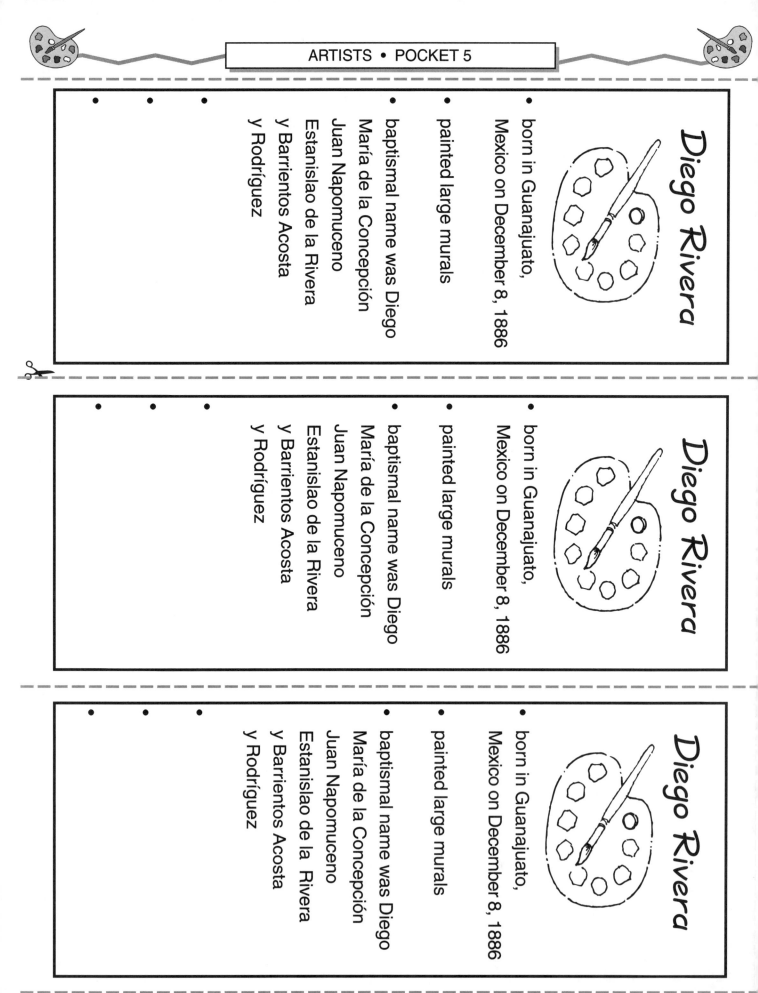

Diego Rivera

- born in Guanajuato, Mexico on December 8, 1886
- painted large murals
- baptismal name was Diego María de la Concepción Juan Napomuceno Estanislao de la Rivera y Barrientos Acosta y Rodríguez

Diego Rivera

- born in Guanajuato, Mexico on December 8, 1886
- painted large murals
- baptismal name was Diego María de la Concepción Juan Napomuceno Estanislao de la Rivera y Barrientos Acosta y Rodríguez

Diego Rivera

- born in Guanajuato, Mexico on December 8, 1886
- painted large murals
- baptismal name was Diego María de la Concepción Juan Napomuceno Estanislao de la Rivera y Barrientos Acosta y Rodríguez

A Mural of Student Life

Materials

- large paper for web
- black marking pen
- pencil
- crayons, colored pencils, marking pens, or poster paint
- 3' (91.5 cm) strip of butcher paper

P.E. *math*

My Day at School

reading *recess*

lunch *spelling*

Steps to Follow

1. Work with students to create a web of things that happen during a normal school day.

2. Students sketch pictures representing these things on the butcher paper. The murals should fill the paper.

3. Use poster paints or colored marking pens to "paint" the mural.

4. When the painting is dry, outline the important shapes with a black marker.

5. Display the murals before you fold them to put them in the pocket.

Another Important Artist

Recognize the creative talents of each student by having them add a pocket of their own to their artists books.

Materials

- artist information bookmark on page 61, reproduced for each student or scanned to be used as a computer template
- pocket label, reproduced from the pattern on page 63

Steps to Follow

1. Model the completion of the artist information bookmark. Demonstrate how to use the template if the computer is being used to complete the bookmark form.

Another Important Artist
Amy Carlon

- born in Walnut Creek, California, on August 31
- loves to draw cats and people
- decorates papers with stencils and tiny drawings
- uses colored pencils, marking pens, and watercolors

2. Have students complete forms about themselves.

3. Students write their names and birthdays on the pocket labels.

4. Students choose samples of their artwork to put in their pockets.

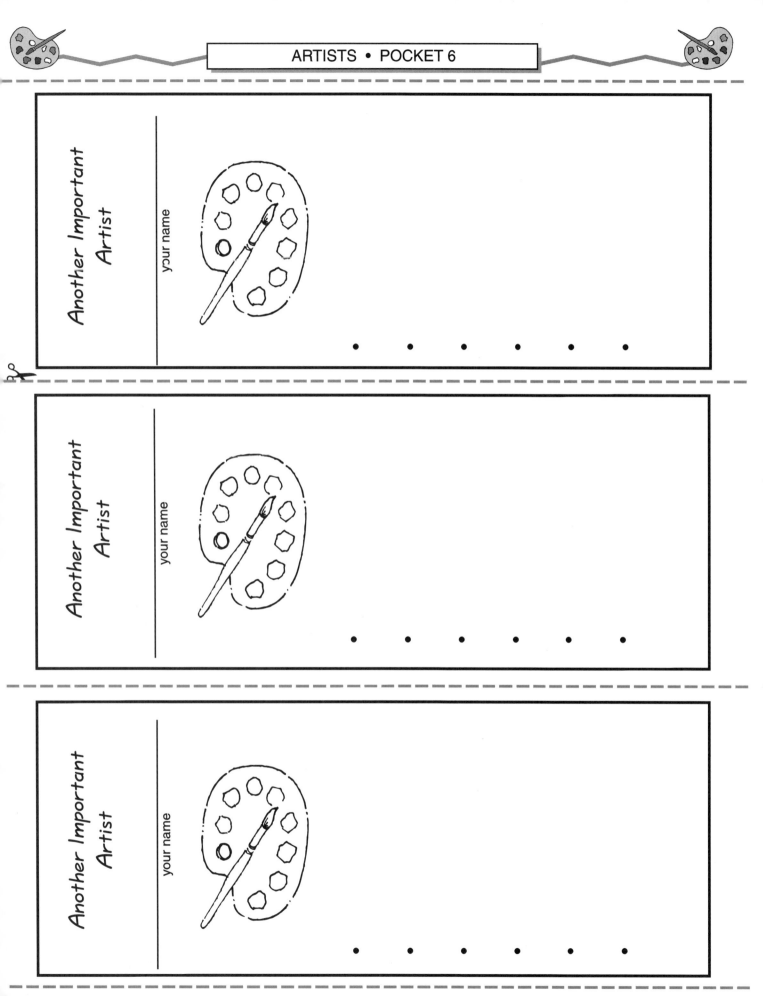

Another Important Artist

your name

Another Important Artist

your name

Another Important Artist

your name

Note: Reproduce this page and page 63 to label each of the six pockets of the Artists book.

Pocket 1

Henri Matisse
1869–1954

Pocket 2

Claude Monet
1840–1926

Pocket 3

Georgia O'Keeffe
1887–1986

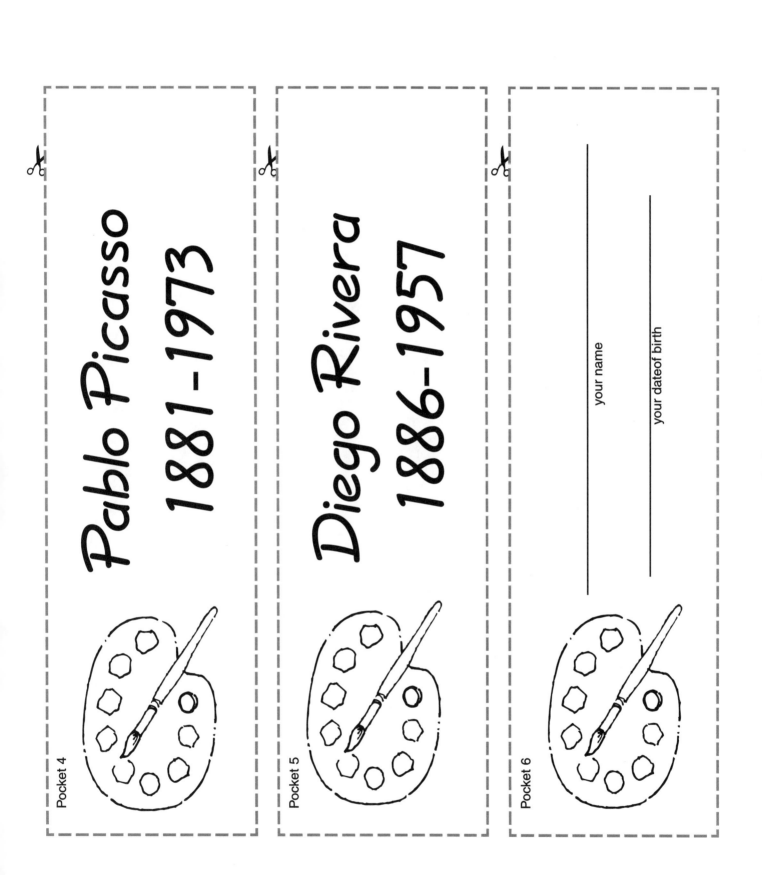

Pocket 4

Pablo Picasso 1881–1973

Pocket 5

Diego Rivera 1886–1957

Pocket 6

your name

your dateof birth

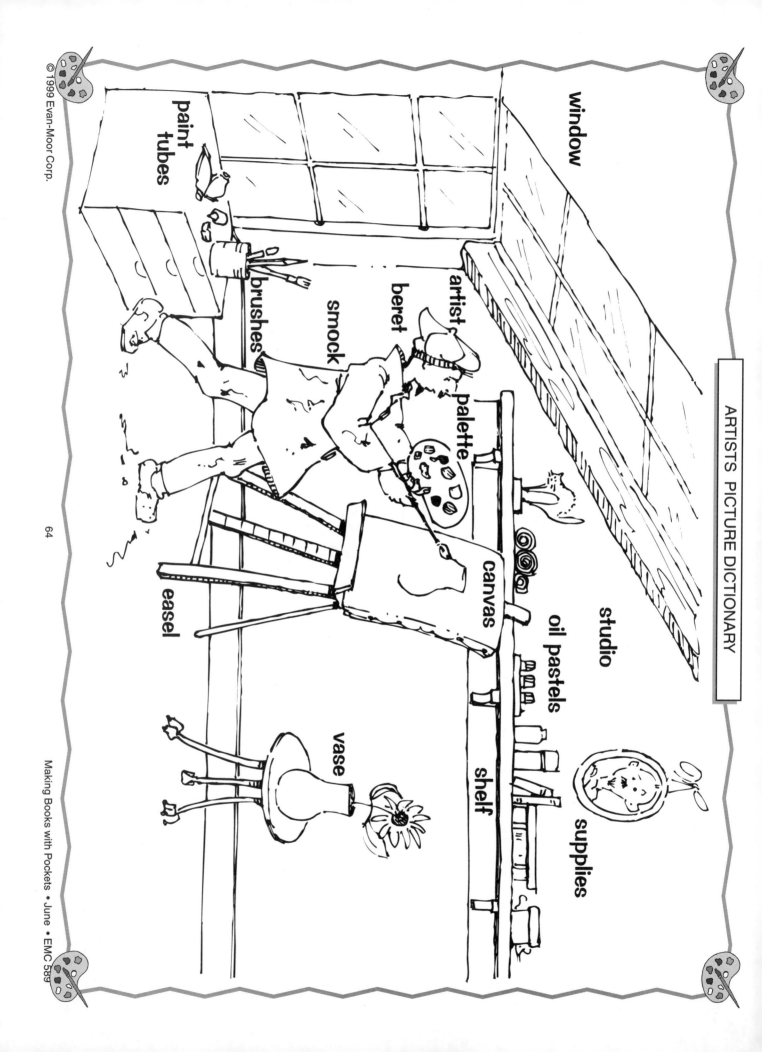

window

paint tubes

brushes

smock

beret

artist

palette

easel

canvas

vase

oil pastels

studio

shelf

supplies

ARTISTS PICTURE DICTIONARY

Name: _____

Farmers Feed Us

Help students understand the important role that farmers play in supplying the world with food. This pocket book supplies information about how food is produced on various kinds of farms. The pockets contain activities that connect this information with your students' lives. Enjoy the creative writing and art projects as you learn.

Farmers Feed Us

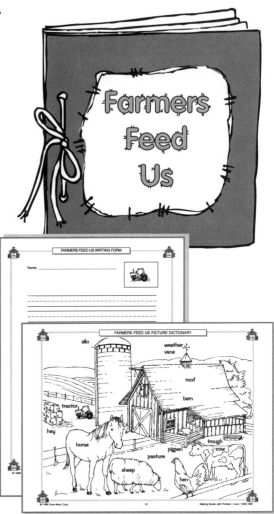

BIBLIOGRAPHY

All Kinds of Farms by Ann Larkin Hansen; ABDO and Daughters, 1996.
Farming by Gail Gibbons; Holiday House, 1988.
Farm Machinery by Ann Larkin Hansen; ABDO and Daughters, 1996.
I Can Be a Farmer by Kathy Henderson; Children's Press, 1989.
If It Weren't For Farmers by Allan Fowler; Children's Press, 1993.
Look Inside a Farm by Alexandra E. Fisher; Grosset and Dunlap, 1994.
Make Me a Peanut Butter Sandwich and a Glass of Milk by Ken Robbins; Scholastic, 1992.
Milk: From Cow to Carton by Aliki; HarperCollins, 1992.
A Visit to the Dairy Farm by Sandra Ziegler; Children's Press, 1987.
Where Food Comes From by Janet Cook and Shirley Bond; Usbourne Publishing, 1989.

Other titles are listed with specific activities.

POCKET 1

Vegetable Book on a Ring
pages 70–72

Create a minibook on a ring that shows many of the different kinds of vegetables that we get from farmers today.

Ear-of-Corn Mosaic
pages 73 and 74

Enjoy the variety of common products that come from corn as you create this ear of corn collage.

Going Bananas
page 75

Reproduce this poem on an overhead transparency and make a copy for each student's pocket. Chant the poem to learn about a banana plantation. Discuss the differences and similarities between a farm in Kansas that grows corn and a plantation in Ecuador that grows bananas.

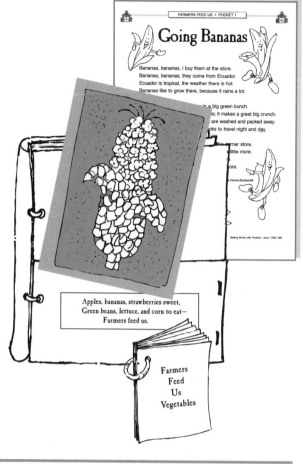

POCKET 2

From Seed to Cereal
pages 76–78

Students create a minibook that illustrates how wheat is planted, harvested, and processed into cereal. Extend this activity by having students write and illustrate a new story in the same pattern, showing how another farm product reaches their tables.

A Loaf of Bread
pages 79–81

Taste different breads and use the experience as an opportunity for student writing. Your students will enjoy writing on slices and then putting the pages together to make a "loaf book." Add a recipe for making an individual loaf of bread.

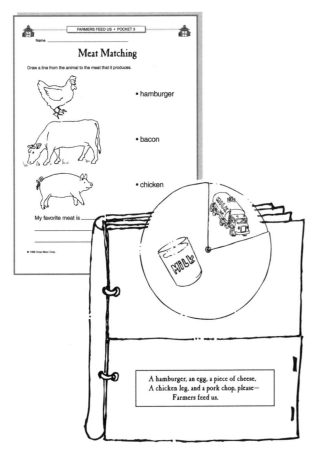

POCKET 3

Milk   pages 82 and 83
Make this wheel to show how milk travels from a dairy farm to the table.

Meat Matching   page 84
Help students match the meats that they eat with the animals that produce them. Complete this activity page and include it in this pocket.

POCKET 4

Many Different Farms   pages 85–88
Create a shape book showing the many different kinds of farms and farmers that help to supply the food that your students eat.

Materials

- 12" (30.5 cm) square of light brown construction paper
- book title patch, reproduced on orange construction paper
- glue

Steps to Follow

1. Tear the edges of the reproduced title to make a patch shape.
2. Glue the patch to the center of the cover.

Vegetable Book-on-a-Ring

Explore the diversity of the vegetables and the farmers that raise them as you create this book-on-a-ring.

Materials

- minibook on pages 71 and 72 reproduced for each student
- 1" metal ring or piece of string
- hole punch

Steps to Follow

1. If possible, bring samples of the vegetables illustrated in the book to show students. Compare the vegetables. Talk about how they grow, which parts are eaten, and whether they are eaten raw or cooked. Try tasting some of the vegetables. Read Janet Stevens's *Tops and Bottoms* (Harcourt Brace,1995) at this point.

2. Have each student cut out the pages for their minibook. Read the information and color the illustrations.

3. Optional: Have students make additional pages on different vegetables for their books.

4. Punch holes in the pages and put them together with the metal ring.

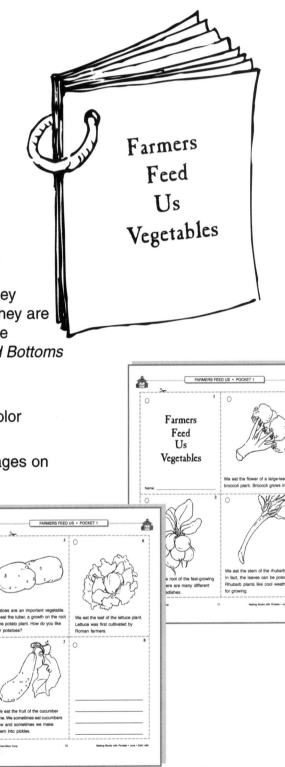

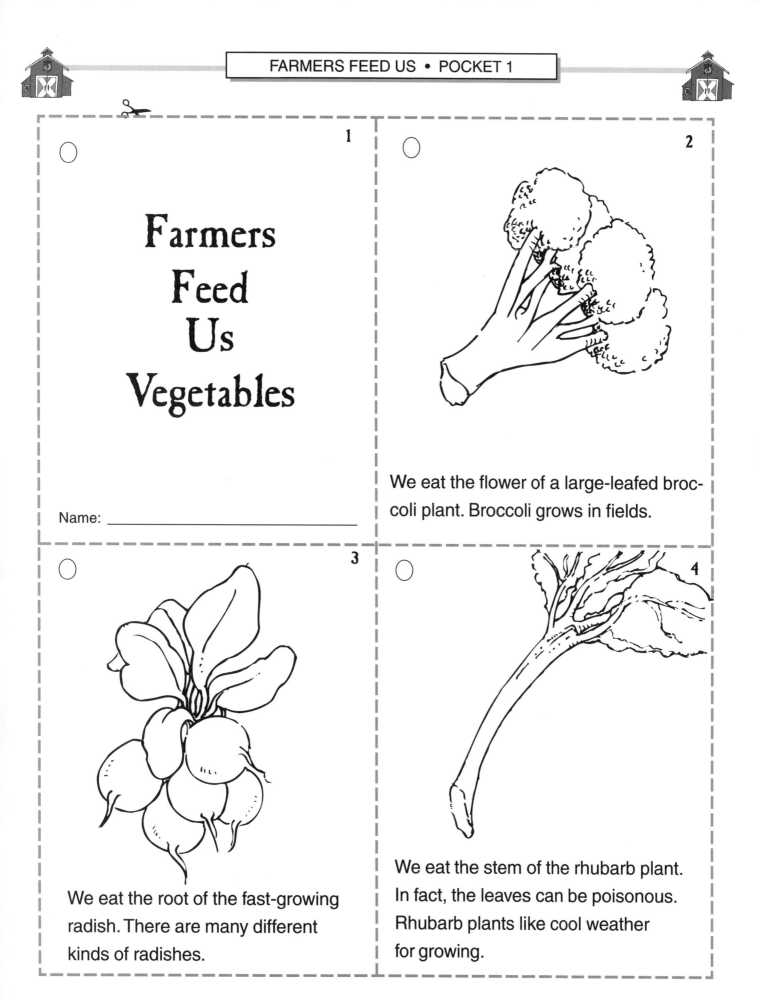

1

Farmers Feed Us Vegetables

Name: _____

2

We eat the flower of a large-leafed broccoli plant. Broccoli grows in fields.

3

We eat the root of the fast-growing radish. There are many different kinds of radishes.

4

We eat the stem of the rhubarb plant. In fact, the leaves can be poisonous. Rhubarb plants like cool weather for growing.

Making Books with Pockets • June • EMC 589

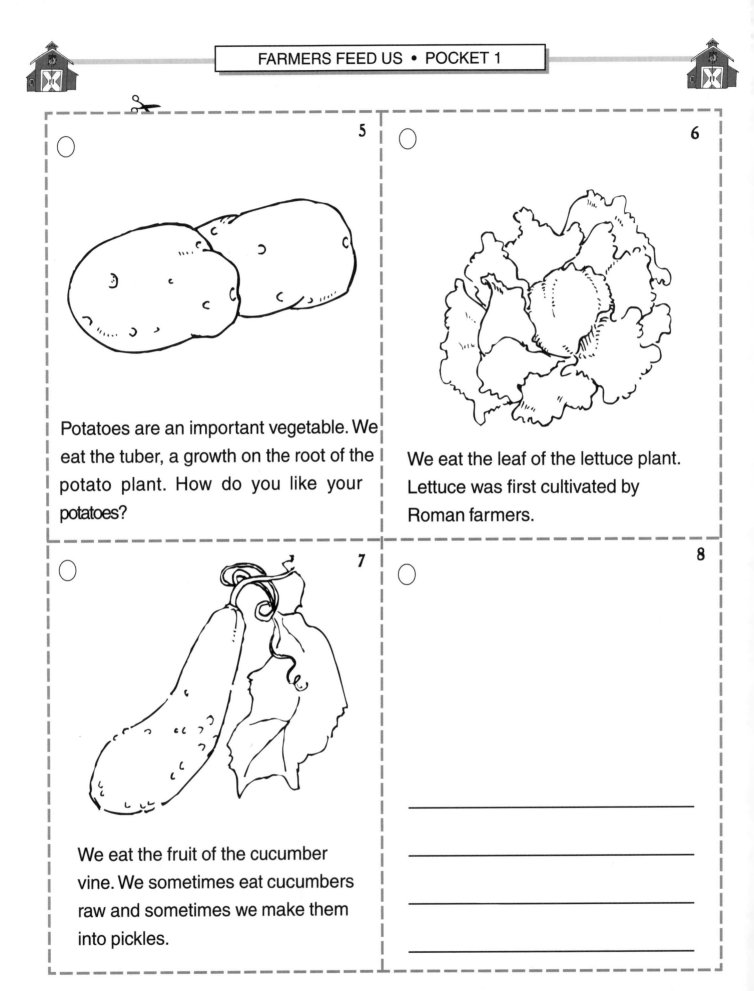

5

Potatoes are an important vegetable. We eat the tuber, a growth on the root of the potato plant. How do you like your potatoes?

6

We eat the leaf of the lettuce plant. Lettuce was first cultivated by Roman farmers.

7

We eat the fruit of the cucumber vine. We sometimes eat cucumbers raw and sometimes we make them into pickles.

8

_____

_____

_____

_____

Ear-of-Corn Mosaic

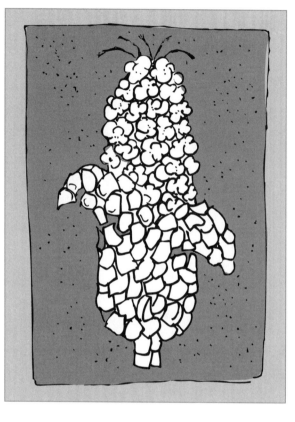

Materials

- ear-of-corn outlines on page 74, reproduced on brown construction paper
- popped popcorn
- cornflakes
- uncooked hominy grits
- cornmeal
- five 2" (5 cm) pieces of brown yarn
- white glue
- 6" x 8" (15 x 20 cm) rectangle of colored posterboard
- stapler

Steps to Follow

1. Cut out the corn along the dotted lines.

2. Direct students to fill the kernel area of the ear of corn with popcorn. Dip each kernel of popped corn into glue and press it to the paper ear. Continue until the area is filled.

3. Using a finger, spread glue over one husk area. Lay cornflakes in the glue. Continue until all husks are filled with cornflakes.

4. Mix cornmeal and grits together. Using your finger, spread glue over the background around the ear of corn. Sprinkle the cornmeal-grits mixture over the glue. Let dry. Dump to remove the extra cornmeal-grits mixture.

5. Make a line of glue on each of the corn silk lines. Place a piece of yarn on each line of the glue.

6. Staple the mosaic onto the posterboard rectangle. Let it dry completely.

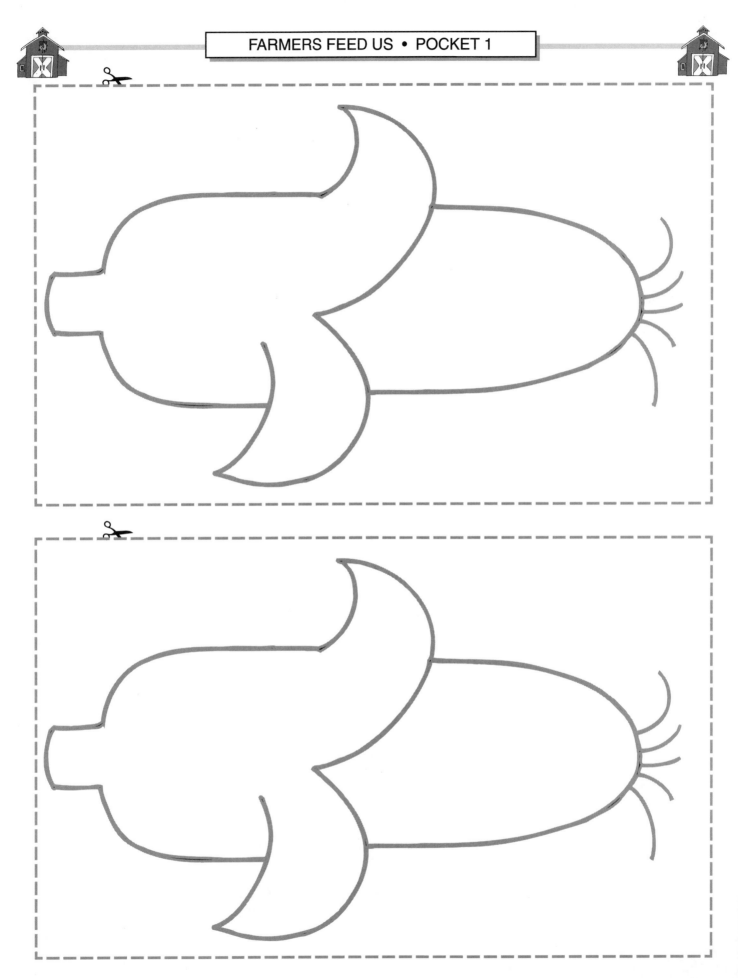

Going Bananas

Bananas, bananas, I buy them at the store.
Bananas, bananas, they come from Ecuador.
Ecuador is tropical, the weather there is hot.
Bananas like to grow there, because it rains a lot.

Bananas on plantations grow in a big green bunch.
The workers cut them off the stems; it makes a great big crunch.
The bunches at the packing plant are washed and packed away.
They're loaded into ships and trucks to travel night and day.

The trucks deliver bananas down to the corner store.
They took two weeks to get there or just a little more.
Bananas, bananas, I buy them at the store.
Bananas, bananas, I always want some more.

Martha Cheney and Diane Hoche Bockwoldt

From Seed to Cereal

An Accordion Book

Flip the book over and paste pictures 4–7 on the back panels.

People all over the world eat grains. Many different kinds of grains are used as cereals or ground into flour. Make this accordion book to learn about one way that wheat is made into cereal.

Materials

- book pages on pages 77 and 78, reproduced for each student.
- 6" x 18" (15 x 45.5 cm) construction paper, any color
- scissors
- glue
- crayons or marking pens

Steps to Follow

1. Read the following books about farming:
   Winter Wheat by Brenda Z. Guiberson; Henry Holt, 1995
   From Wheat to Pasta by Robert Egan; Children's Press, 1997
   Cereal, Nuts & Spices by Cecilia Fitzsimmons; Julian Messner, 1997

2. Help students to describe, in their own words, the cycle of raising and harvesting food crops. List their ideas on the chalkboard.

3. Make an accordion book to show the steps that wheat goes through before it becomes cereal on the breakfast table.
   - Color the illustrations on the book pages and cut them out.
   - Accordion-fold the construction paper strip into fourths.
   - Paste the pictures in order on the front and back of the strip.

4. Read the cereal story.

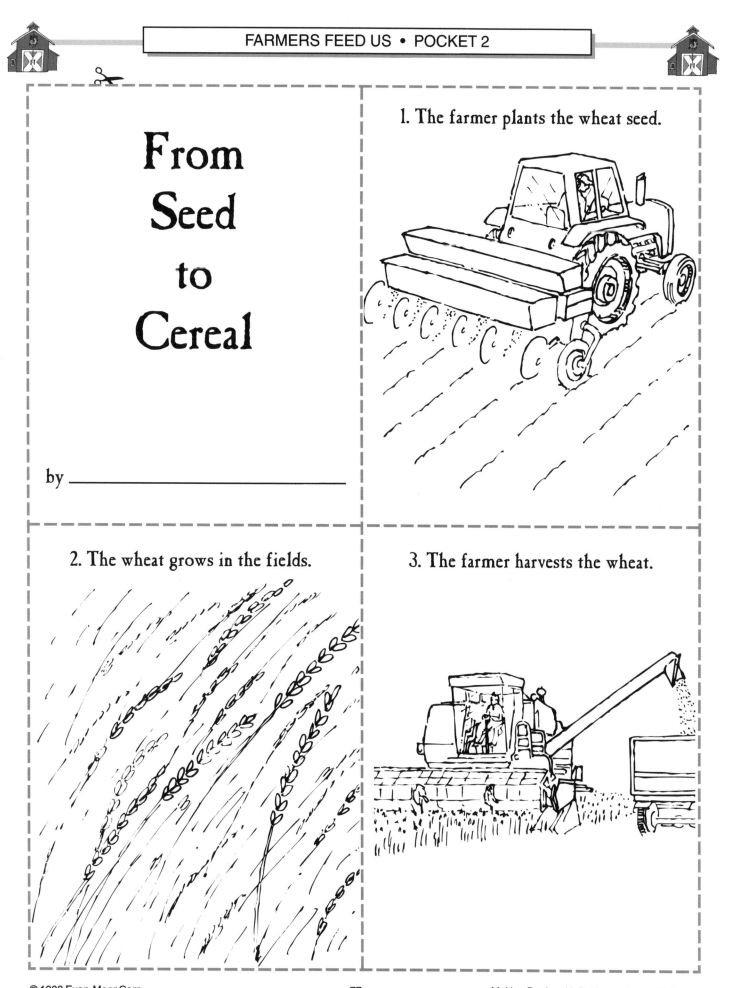

From Seed to Cereal

by _____

1. The farmer plants the wheat seed.

2. The wheat grows in the fields.

3. The farmer harvests the wheat.

Making Books with Pockets • June • EMC 589

4. The wheat is sold to a factory.

5. The factory makes the wheat into cereal.

6. The cereal is sold to a grocery store.

Toasty Flakes
Toasty Flakes
Toasty Flakes

7. I eat the cereal for breakfast.

Cereal

Making Books with Pockets • June • EMC 589

A Loaf of Bread

People all over the world eat breads of many kinds. Taste different kinds of bread and then create this loaf-shaped book to record your experiences.

Materials

- several different kinds of bread for tasting
- several slice patterns on page 80, reproduced for each student
- bread recipe on page 81, reproduced for each student.
- paper fastener

Steps to Follow

1. Bring samples of different breads to class. You may want to ask students to bring in samples of breads that they like. Bring in several unusual kinds yourself. Be sure to include flat breads as well as yeast breads.

2. Spend some time comparing the breads. Have the students use one of the slice pages to record words that you use to describe the breads. Then make a Bread Word Bank. If you have a digital camera, take photos of the different breads to use as illustrations for writing experiences.

3. Cut the breads into tiny pieces and taste the different breads. Compare the breads again. Add some "taste" words to your word bank. Students might use another slice page to tell about their favorites. This is an excellent opportunity to make a class graph showing favorites.

5. Write more about bread. Give lots of suggestions, but let your students choose their own genre. Suggest that they use their Bread Word Banks as they write.
   - Write a poem about how bread smells as it is baking.
   - Write an essay on the importance of bread around the world.
   - Write a story about the last slice left in the bread box.

6. Gather all of the slice pages and the bread recipe, make a cover using another slice, and hook your pages together into a bread book, using a paper fastener.

Pattern for Bread Slice

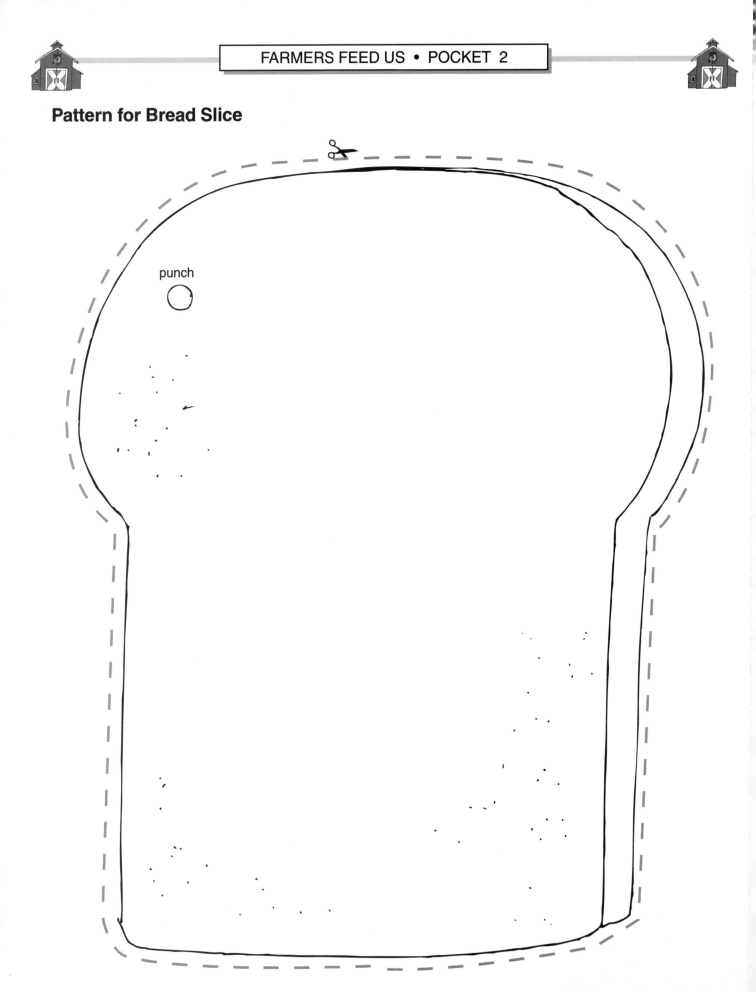

punch

Baking Bread

Ingredients

- yeast
- honey
- warm water
- cooking oil
- evaporated milk
- white flour
- whole wheat flour

Equipment

- measuring spoons and cups
- bowls for mixing
  (the size of a cereal bowl is fine)
- aluminum foil miniloaf pan
- flat surface for kneading
- plastic wrap
- oven

Steps to Follow

1. Dissolve 2 teaspoons (8 g) of yeast and 4 teaspoons (20 ml) of honey in ¼ cup (60 ml) of warm water. Stir until well mixed.

2. Add 4 teaspoons (20 ml) of oil, ¼ cup (60 ml) of evaporated milk, and ½ cup (63 g) of white flour. Stir until combined.

3. Measure about ½ cup (63 g) of whole wheat flour. Add just enough to form a ball.

4. Knead the dough for 5 minutes. Roll the dough into a ball. Put the ball into the pan.

5. Cover the dough loosely with plastic wrap and let it rise for about 30 minutes.

6. Bake the miniloaf in a 350° F (177° C) oven for about 22 minutes.

Milk

Most of the milk we drink comes from dairy cows. Make this wheel to trace the steps from a farm to your grocery store.

Susie

Materials

- two 6" (15 cm) circles cut from an old file folder

  Note: It's easiest if the teacher or parent helper cuts these circles prior to the activity. One circle will need to have a wedge-shaped window cut from it. Either make a template so that students can cut the window or cut it out when cutting all the circles.

- wheel pictures on page 83
- 5" (13 cm) square writing paper
- paper fastener
- scissors
- glue
- crayons or marking pens

Steps to Follow

1. Read a book about how milk is made such as *Milk: From Cow to Carton* by Aliki; HarperCollins, 1992 or *The Milk Makers* by Gail Gibbons; Aladdin, 1987. Talk about milk's journey from dairy farm to grocery store.

2. Color the illustrations on the milk wheel on page 83. Cut out the wheel and glue it to one file folder circle.

3. Use the template to cut a wedge out of the other file folder circle.

4. Stack the circles. The circle with the window will be on top.

5. Put the paper fastener through the center of the two circles.

6. Turn the top circle to view the process.

7. Have students write a description of the process. Attach the written description to the back of the wheel.

8. Glue the milk glass to the top wheel.

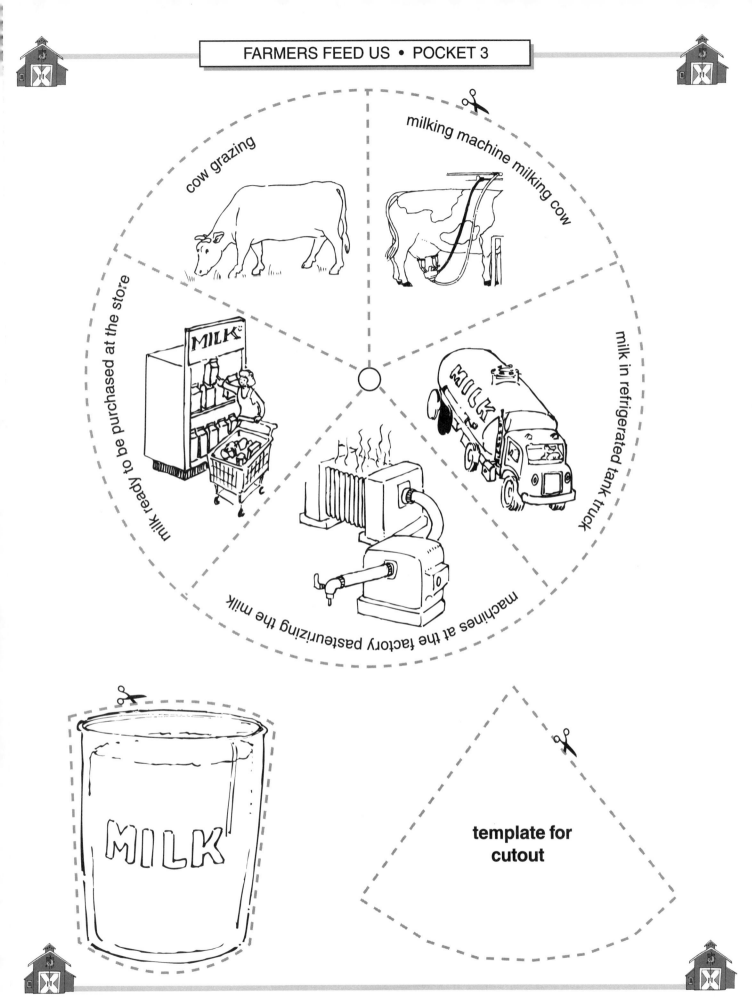

cow grazing

milking machine milking cow

milk in refrigerated tank truck

machines at the factory pasteurizing the milk

milk ready to be purchased at the store

MILK

template for
cutout

Name _____

Meat Matching

Draw a line from the animal to the meat that it produces.

• hamburger

• bacon

• drumstick

My favorite meat is _____

_____

_____.

Many Different Farms

Encourage your students to recognize the many different kinds of farms that help feed us. Create pages for this barn-shaped book for each farm you discover.

Materials

- barn template and writing form on page 86, six for each student
- barn door patterns on page 87
- construction paper
  barn front—red, 9"x 12" (23 x 30.5 cm)
- black marking pen
- writing paper
- farm pictures on pages 88, reproduced for each student
- hole punch
- rafia
- glue

Steps to Follow

1. Cut out the six barn writing forms.

2. Use one writing form as a template. Trace the barn shape on the red construction paper. Cut it out.

3. Add the roof line with black marking pen.

4. Color and cut out the barn door and interior view patterns.

5. Glue the barn doors to the interior view where indicated. Now paste the whole door piece to the front of the barn.

6. Paste the hayloft door to the front of the barn.

7. Cut apart the farm pictures on page 88. Glue one to each writing form. Write about a different kind of farm on each barn-shaped writing page.

8. Stack the pages of your barn book behind the cover. Punch a hole at the top of the barn and secure with a rafia bow.

**Barn Template
and
Writing Form**

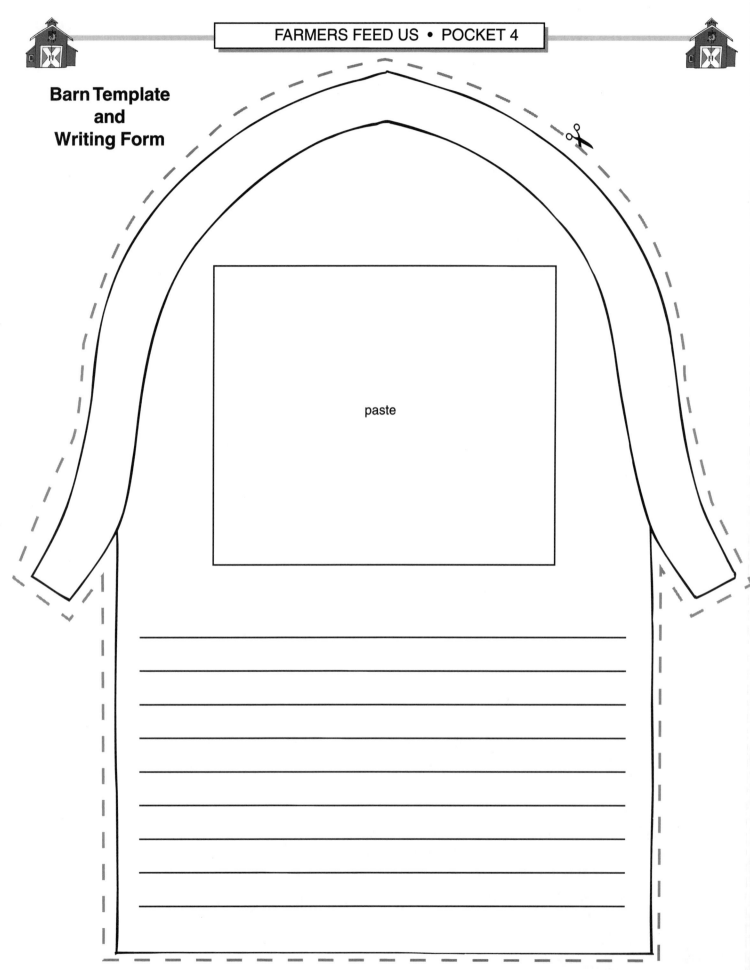

paste

Making Books with Pockets • June • EMC 589

Barn Door Patterns

paste

paste

Name: _____

dairy farm

egg farm

cattle ranch

rice paddy

orange grove

banana plantation

Note: Reproduce this page and page 91 to label each of the four pockets of the Farmers Feed Us Book.

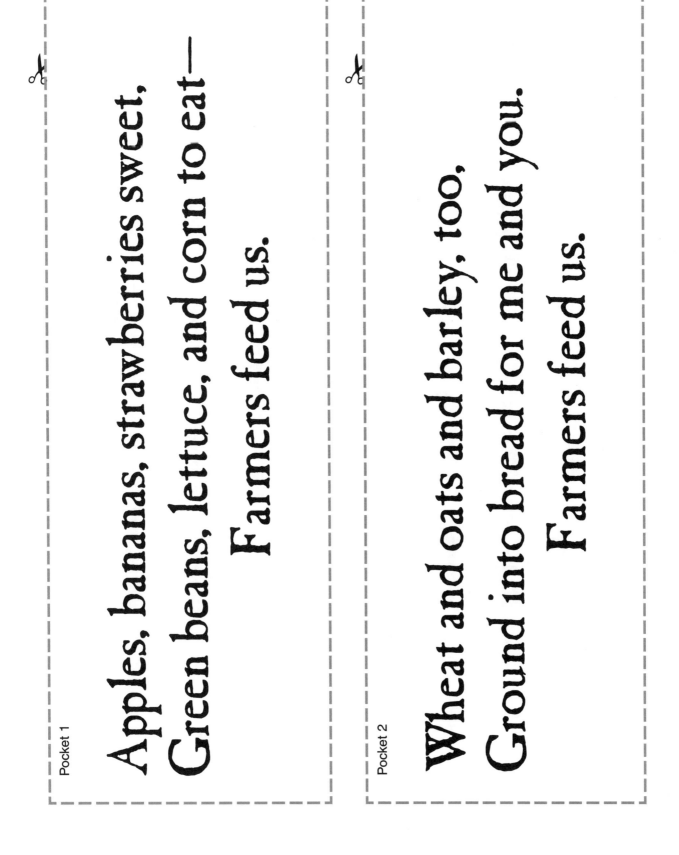

Pocket 1

Apples, bananas, strawberries sweet,
Green beans, lettuce, and corn to eat—
Farmers feed us.

Pocket 2

Wheat and oats and barley, too,
Ground into bread for me and you.
Farmers feed us.

Pocket 3

A hamburger, an egg, a piece of cheese,
A chicken leg, and a pork chop, please—
Farmers feed us.

Pocket 4

Breakfast at home, dinner at a cafe—
Farmers grow what we eat every day.
Farmers feed us.

weather vane

roof

barn

silo

trough

cow

pigpen

hen

pasture

sheep

tractor

hay

horse

Making Eooks with Pockets • June • EMC 589

FARMERS FEED US WRITING FORM

Name: ______________________________

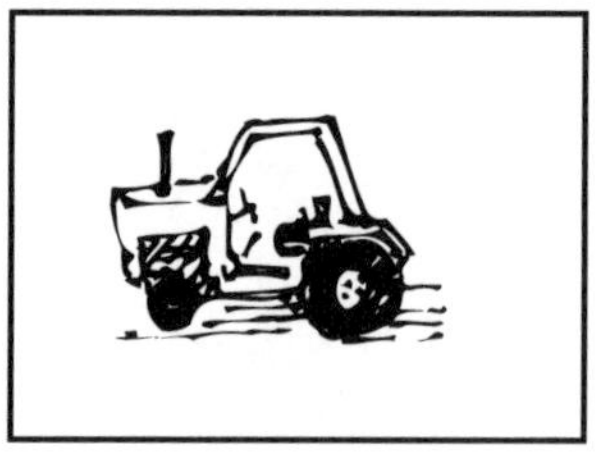

Bulletin Board
Bonanza

Hanging Together—page 94

Color the baby sloths and use them as a base for classroom interactive activities such as showing the words that combine to make contractions and compound words or the numbers in math problems.

Suggested Contractions			Compound Words		
can	not	can't	rainforest	rain	forest
will	not	won't	butterfly	butter	fly
I	am	I'm	understory	under	story
we	are	we're	anteater	ant	eater
are	not	aren't	hummingbird	humming	bird
we	will	we'll	riverbank	river	bank
she	will	she'll	riverbed	river	bed
he	will	he'll			

From Farm to Table—page 96

This "table" is filled with foods from many different kinds of farms. Label each food with a tag, reproduced using the pattern below.

Tag for Labeling the Packages

From Farm to Table

_____

_____

_____

Hanging Together

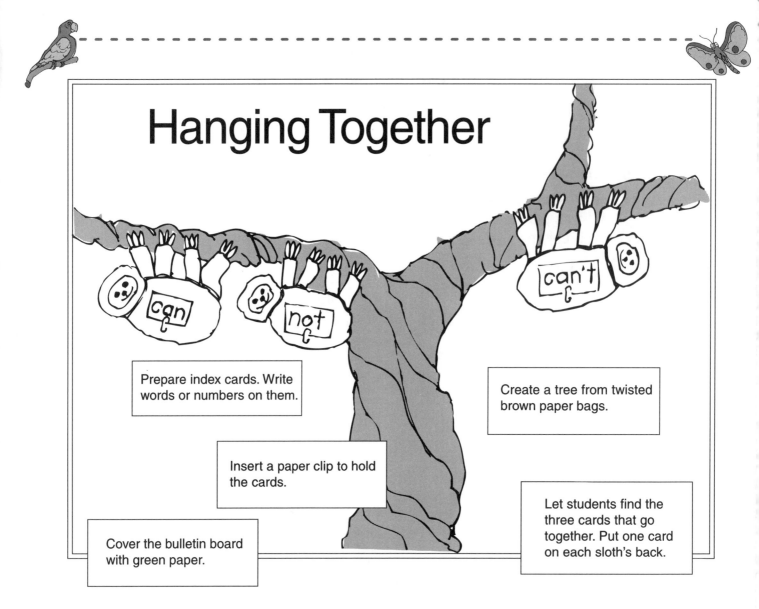

Prepare index cards. Write words or numbers on them.

Create a tree from twisted brown paper bags.

Insert a paper clip to hold the cards.

Let students find the three cards that go together. Put one card on each sloth's back.

Cover the bulletin board with green paper.

Materials

- baby sloth patterns on page 95, reproduced on brown construction paper
- construction paper for each sloth face—white, 3" x 2" (7.5 x 5 cm) claws—four gray, 2" (5 cm) squares
- black marking pen
- glue
- scissors
- brown paper bags
- green butcher paper
- paper clips
- index cards

How to Make Sloths

1. Cut out sloths.

2. Tear around the edges of the white paper to make the sloth faces.

3. Add facial details with a black marking pen.

4. Cut each gray square to make three-clawed feet.

5. Glue the face and the claws onto the sloth.

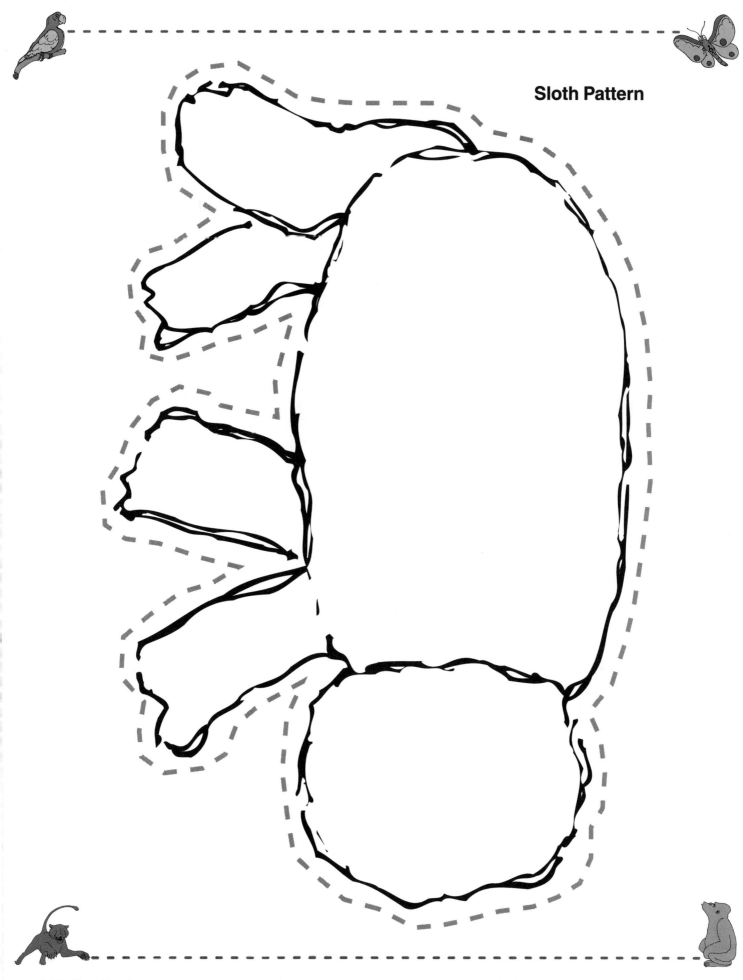

Sloth Pattern

Making Books with Pockets • June • EMC 589

From Farm to Table

Cover your bulletin board with the tablecloth.

Collect packages and containers to represent different foods.

Materials

- red-and-white-checkered tablecloth
- containers from food items
- reproduced copies of the tag shown on page 93

Make a tag for each food container that tells about the farm where the food may have come from.

For example:
The milk I put on my cereal comes from a dairy farm in Longmont.

Attach a tag to each food package and hang it on the board.

Making Books with Pockets • June • EMC 589